Almost Home

Embracing The Magical Connection
Between Positive Humor & Spirituality

Jacki Kwan LCSW-C

02 03 04 05 HH 10 9 8 7 6 5 4 3 2 1
Printed in the United States of America
ISBN: 0-9715739-1-3
Library of Congress Control #: 2002100148

Requests for permission to make copies of any part of
this work can be made to:

Jacki@HAHALOGY.com
fax: 301-907-4610
or visit: www.HAHALOGY.com

Published by
Cameo Publications
6213 Jerome Blvd.
Harrisburg, PA 17112
phone: 717-651-5354
fax: 717-651-5235

publisher@cameopublications.com
www.cameopublications.com

Dedication

I dedicate this book to Alex, Jen, and Brian, my precious family.

To Alex, my husband, who has hung in there with me through all of my heretofore seemingly disconnected endeavors and who has been by my side through my darkest hours and celebrated my growth.

To Jen, my favorite daughter, who has shown me courage in the face of darkness and has developed a sense of humor to which to aspire. You have beauty inside and out!

To Brian, my favorite son, who has been wonderfully honest with me about me. You have given me so many "Brianisms" that I cherish. You are a true mensh, mon fils.

All three of you have saluted me with groans "that ate Chicago" for my relentless punning!! I love you. I am so blessed!

About The Author

Jacki Kwan is a Licensed Certified Social Worker at the Clinical Level, a Master Practitioner of Neuro-linguistic Programming, a Registered Laughter Leader with the World Laughter Tour™, and a Therapeutic Clown. She leads Laughter Club sessions at nursing homes and assisted living facilities in the Washington, DC area.

She has been presenting workshops on humor and health since 1994. In 1999, she created HA!HA!LOGY®, a multi-faceted therapeutic humor program for health care facilities, which is now in place at the Hebrew Home of Greater Washington in Rockville, MD.

Jacki is the wife of Alex Kwan, M.D. and the mother of two awesome adults, Jenifer and Brian. She is a friend to many and a funny person. Her license plate reads: "LUV2LAF." After traveling to China with Patch Adams and 44 other clowns in September 2000, Jacki solidified her mission to change the world one "ha" at a time.

Acknowledgments

I have a lifetime of family, friends, teachers, and acquaintances who all have impacted my life and have let me know that I'm Almost Home. My mother always said that everyone has a book in them. Thanks, Mom..............here is mine! You always said that I could do whatever I set my mind to. I've taken you to heart. I love you.

In the nuts and bolts arena, I cannot say thank you enough to Dawn and Dave Josephson of Cameo Publications who made this happen. What a team! They have given shape and voice to this project in a most pleasant and efficient way. Bless you both.

I searched a year and a half for the right people to create my brochure. Not only did John and Kristen Vorhes design a magnificent brochure, but they also have continued to guide me with humor and professionalism as the cover for this book was designed. Bless you both!

A gazillian thanks to my daughter, Jen, who proofread the final manuscript.

I want to thank Joel Goodman for creating The HUMOR Project in Saratoga Springs, NY and opening my eyes to the wonderful world of therapeutic humor.

Allen Klein, you are a mentor and friend. Your encouragement along the way has kept me going when I was ready to give up.

Without you, Leslie Gibson, I would not have had a model for HA!HA!LOGY®. Your most generous spirit opened many doors for me and I thank you for that! You also introduced me to Steve Wilson, who created The World Laughter Tour.

I'm sure in one of my other lives that you, Steve Wilson, were my twin brother! My learning from you doesn't stop. You have a way of injecting humor at the perfect time to help me get a fresh perspective. You are a gift.

To Lee Berk, DrPH CHES FACSM, thank you for scientific documentation in the land of laughter as medicine.

It was Patch Adams, M.D. who provided a focus for me. Our trip to China with the 44 other clowns helped me see that being a clown is a very noble profession indeed. I cannot thank you enough.

A special thank you to Jewel Thompson and Julie Lundy for providing a cozy nest in which HA!HA!LOGY could hatch.

I want to say a few special words about the folks at The Hebrew Home of Greater Washington in Rockville, MD. Your open minds and hearts have given HA!HA!LOGY a wonderful home.

Finally, I am so grateful for my many, many clown friends whose kindred spirits live within me every breathing moment! I love you all!

Contents

Foreword

It has been said that most people die with their dreams still inside them. Thank goodness Jacki Kwan is alive and making her dreams come true.

This wonderful book documents Jacki's journey – from a phone call seeking a humor mentor, to a clowning trip to China, to caring and cajoling with folks in a nursing home. This book is also an inspiration for all of us not to give up and not to let our dream die within us.

Read this book. In these trying times, we all need Kwan and her message more than ever.

–Allen Klein,
author of *The Courage to Laugh and
The Healing Power of Humor*

Preface

In the wake of the September 11, 2001 terrorist attacks, I am even more aware of our need for joy. We all have the capacity for joy. For some reason, many of us are not connected to our precious selves enough to know it. I don't mean to discount pain…I have had more than my fair share of that in my life. I'm talking about balancing the joy and sorrow so the scales won't tip so far in a negative direction. An overabundance of negativity breeds dis-ease.

During this time, I have become thankful for who I am. Gratitude. Gratitude. Gratitude. I hope and pray that reading this book will inspire hope in each and every one of you to follow your gut and become who you want to be. There's a lot of wisdom inside each of us…all we have to do is trust our intuition without all of the collective negative messages that we may we have received in the past.

There is, I believe, some force "out there" that's bigger and greater than we are. I haven't used the word God specifically in this book (maybe that's for the next one). This book is, however, all about Her nature. I know She's alive and well inside and all around me. I didn't always know that. So I share that very special spirit with you, whatever you choose to call it.

That spirit is here. I invite you to take it, embrace it, and trust it.

Chapter One  Home Is Where The Spirit Is

"You are led through your lifetime by the inner learning creature, the playful spiritual being that is your real self."
– Richard Bach

I had my first glimpse of "home" in 1981. It occurred when I was diagnosed with having an ovarian cyst. My doctor informed me that I needed surgery to either drain or remove the cyst, and I consented to the procedure. Prior to my surgery date, I met with the medical staff so I could review and sign all the paperwork. With my signature, I acknowledged all the risks that could present themselves during surgery, and I even gave my consent for the doctor to perform a total hysterectomy should that be the only course of action once they opened me up.

When the day of the surgery arrived, I had no idea what would happen to me or whether or not I'd wake up with all my parts still intact. As I laid on the gurney in the cold hospital hall, a million thoughts raced through my head. I was terrified of surgery, but I had no choice. Thoughts of my two beautiful children, Jenifer and Brian, and my husband Alex, dominated my mind. I was terrified that I may never wake up from the anesthesia – a point my anesthesiologist husband told me was unlikely. If that did happen, though, how would my family get along without me?

I was also fearful of the possibility of having a total hysterectomy. How would I handle it if the very essence of my womanhood was suddenly gone? One terrible scenario after another played itself out in my head. Needless to say, I was a terrible patient. With each awful thought my blood pressure rose and my pulse quickened until the nurse on duty begged me to relax. Easy for her to say! I could have used some humor to lighten the situation.

Try as I might, I could not calm myself. I prayed that they'd wheel me into the operating room soon and put me under. I didn't know how much longer I could handle the stress of my impending surgery without driving myself crazy or at least into a state of hyperventilation. Finally, after what seemed like hours of lying in the cold hall but was actually only a few minutes, an attendant wheeled me into the operating room. The anesthesiologist started my IV, and my eyes inadvertently closed.

As I lay there, I felt the mechanical nature of the procedure take place: Roll the patient over, undo the hospital gown, cover the patient with a sterile robe, thrust the patient's legs into the stirrups. I knew that they weren't supposed to do any of these activities until I was asleep, so I decided I needed to let them know immediately that the anesthesia hadn't taken effect yet. I tried to open my eyes, but they wouldn't respond. Just then, my mouth opened, but not because I made it happen. Someone was shoving an airway into my mouth. I felt the cold plastic descend into my windpipe and my airway close around it. I heard the doctors and nurses talk about the procedure and the tools and the possible "first incision."

I wanted to yell, flail my arms, kick my legs, or do anything that would let them know I was still awake, but it was too late. They had already begun the curare drip, which prohibits bodily movement during surgery, and my entire body was paralyzed even though my brain and senses were still wide-awake.

So there I lay – awake and fully conscious – but unable to stop the doctors from cutting me open and possibly killing me. Fear overtook every inch of my body. "I'm going to die," I said to myself over and over. "I know I'm going to die." Images of my life rushed in front of me. I saw pictures from my childhood – my fifth birthday party, my Confirmation, my first day of high school. I saw my wedding day and the birth of each of my children. I relived every major memory that my brain had stored. "They can't let me die," I shouted inside. The more I struggled, though, the more I knew there was no hope. Each attempt to move only made me more frightened. After a few more moments of fighting, I finally arrived at the point where I realized there was nothing I could do. I had no control; I had to let go.

At that moment of total release, the tunnel appeared. I immediately knew it was the tunnel everyone who has had near death experiences talks about. The tunnel materialized not above me, but right at waist level. It was long and dark, and at the end of the tunnel was bright light – the brightest light I ever remember seeing. Even though the light was nearly blinding, it didn't hurt my eyes and I refused to turn my head away. The warmth emanating from the light felt peaceful and serene.

I let the light's glow envelop my body. I felt it permeate every pore of my being, and I willingly began to follow it to the tunnel's end. The closer I got to the light, the greater the feelings of peace and serenity became. I wanted nothing more than to bask in the light's glow for eternity. It was the most wonderful experience I can recall.

Just as quickly as the light appeared, it began to diminish. "NO!" I thought to myself. "It can't go. I have to get to it." I tried forcing myself towards what remained of the light, but an unseen force was pulling me back. It was like a giant rubber band stretched to its limit was roped around my waist and repelling me backwards. Moments later, I was waking up in the recovery room. My surgery was over, my cyst was drained, and all my body parts were right where they should be.

Although I was happy to have gotten through the surgery unharmed, I was also saddened. Seeing that light was the most amazing experience of my life, and now it was gone. I know that seeing the light meant I was within moments of dying, but I didn't care. I wanted nothing more than to feel that light's warmth on me forever. As I lay in the recovery room I vowed to myself that I would find a way to bring that light into my life so I wouldn't have to wait until I died to feel it again.

While I was in the light, I felt as if my spirit was totally free. I felt as if my inner energy was a part of something larger than myself. For once in my life, there were no control issues; no fear, no sadness, no depression, nothing negative at all. All I felt was positive energy and a sense of goodness and well being.

That fateful day in 1981 changed my life forever. I knew I had to find a way to bring that white light into my life so I wouldn't have to wait until I died to feel that way again. At that point, I had no clue as to how to make that happen. After the surgery, life went on as normal (whatever that means) – each day I was trying to discover the steps to take to rekindle that light in my life.

A few months later, as I sat home in my living room, I began thinking about my life and the various choices I made along the way. At this point I was still searching for that special calling that would ignite my life force. As I reviewed my life's course of events, it came to me: If I wanted to know what to do with my future, I'd have to look back at my past. If I wanted my spirit to feel free and alive, I'd have to examine my life and uncover what made my spirit soar as a child. Only then could I recapture the spirituality I felt I was missing and so desperately wanted to experience.

So that day I took my first step towards one of my many journeys home. What I learned and discovered changed my life for the better…forever.

All Roads Lead to Home

What is "home"?

For most people, "home" is a physical dwelling that houses their family and personal possessions. Home is ideally filled with love and understanding. Home is the familiar smells and sounds and images and feelings that can comfort a weary body and mind after a long day. Home can be the one place where people feel truly comfortable...or it can be the one place they dread and fear. The image of "home" evokes different images and feelings in each of us.

I've had many different "homecomings" in my life, and they've each impacted me in a profound way. But first, let me explain that for me, "home" has many different connotations.

First, "home" is myself – my inner being. It's my spirit within that reaches out to others and connects with them on a level that can be felt and not always outwardly seen. For many years I was afraid to come "home." I didn't know how to be comfortable with myself, so to me, "home" was not a comforting place.

"Home" also refers to my Jewish faith and the Hebrew Home of Greater Washington where I use Humor Therapy to ease people's suffering. When I was a little girl, my grandmother was a resident at the Hebrew Home. The home had an Orthodox Synagogue on premises, so that was where my parents and I would go for services. After my grandmother died, when I was nine years old, my parents stopped visiting the Hebrew Home and joined a Reform congregation, which is the least traditional in the Jewish religion. It was at the Reform temple that I began to feel "less than" because I didn't feel that I was accepted by many of the kids in my religious school classes – the so-called "in" crowd. At that point, I began to associate those negative emotions with my Jewish faith. I denied my Jewish background for many decades, and it took an act of faith for me to reclaim my Jewish heritage and return to the Hebrew Home, which I'll talk more about in chapter two.

Finally, "home" is the place where my spirit resides when it's not in my physical body. For years now I've been fascinated with the work of Sylvia Browne, a working psychic for over forty years. She frequently talks about "home" as being the place our spirits go when they're not on this earth – a sort of "heaven," if you will. Sylvia Browne and other psychics believe that we all exist in another dimension as spiritual beings, and we come to earth at our own will with the goal of learning specific lessons. When our physical life on earth is over, we return to our true "home" on the other side where we can assimilate the knowledge we've gained in all our lifetimes and use it to help our spiritual selves grow. After much reading, research, and personal experience, I've come to embrace the psychics' concept of "home" and consider it an integral part of my faith, mission, and spirituality.

It's only in the past few years that I've begun to find my way "home" – in every sense of the word. My work as a Humor Therapist has been the thread that has woven together the various aspects of my life and what is making my home complete.

The more I work as a Humor Therapist, the more I believe that humor has the ability to connect people on a spiritual level. When I refer to humor, I define it broadly. To me, humor is a positive state of mind, and people need different things at different times in order to be in "good humor." Sometimes we need to laugh, while other times we simply need someone to sit and breathe with us. Humor, as it pertains to Humor Therapy, is never hurtful nor does it degrade a person's spirit. It's always uplifting and positive, and it gives people a temporary release of any negativity they are harboring.

I've had the privilege of working with a number of incredible residents at the Hebrew Home – people with dementia, people with Alzheimer's disease, people with cancer, people who are dying. In each of them I've seen that "spark" of life – their inner force that, despite their illness, can't be broken. Even if the people were too far-gone physically to speak or move, that spark – the essence of their spirituality – has come alive during a Humor Therapy session. I've seen firsthand how intimately related humor and spirituality really are.

What is Spirtuality?

I believe that spirituality is the concept of our true selves without the ego. It's the essence of who we are. I believe that the spirit is temporarily enclosed in our physical bodies and that it acts as our life force while we are here on earth.

Babies and children are most in touch with their spirituality because they are closer to the time when they came from "home." So, as adults, spirituality is the kid within, that sense of creativity, that non-judgmental part of us that is all encompassing. Spirituality is all those non-tangible parts of who we are. And I believe it's that spirit that connects us to other people and to all creatures, both those that are still among us and those that have already passed on and returned "home." In essence, our spirituality is our connection to something bigger and greater than ourselves.

Humor is an excellent way to trigger the spiritual connection between people. Humor and the act of laughing transcend all language barriers and give people a common ground on which we all can relate. Wayne Dyer, a modern day philosopher and motivational speaker, frequently talks about the sound of "ah" and how that "ah" sound appears in our spiritual beings' names like God, Yahweh, Buddha, and Allah. His words got me thinking, and I realized that the sound of laughter also has the "ah" sound in it. Yes, the sound of laughter has the same spiritual sound as God or Allah. In fact, if you turn "ha" around, you get "ah" – Aaaaa – the sound of wonder. So laughter is indeed a spiritual experience. And when two people laugh together, their spirits have the opportunity to connect and comfort each other. What could be more spiritual than that?

A Journey of Discovery

I went to my first Humor Conference in 1994. The events leading up to that conference as well as the resulting experiences and their impact on my spiritual journey are worth retelling. In the years that have preceded, I've learned a great deal about smiles and laughter and their impact on the human spirit. I've also learned that humor can connect us to each other in ways we never dreamed possible.

My work today reminds me of a song from the 60s that Dionne Warwick sang called "What the World Needs Now." The lyrics go something like this:

What the world needs now
is love, sweet love.
That's the only thing that there's just too little of.
No, not just for some, but for everyone."

That song is sort of like my motto, only I substitute the word "laugh" whenever there is "love" in the lyrics. I know without a doubt that love and laughter are intimately intertwined and that sharing laughter is an absolutely "love-ly" thing to do.

Today I invite you to join me on my journey and to discover how humor, smiles, and laughter can make an impact on your life and on the lives of those you know. It's a journey you won't soon forget…and one that has the power to change your whole outlook on life.

So get ready…Get set…And let's Rock and Roll!

Chapter Two

The Road Home

"Choose a job you love and you will never have to work a day in your life."– Confucius

Humor is a wonderful way to cope with stress, and I've been stressed out since before I was born. My mother's pregnancy with me was not planned, and add to that, I was born two months early. By today's standards, being two months premature is not a life-threatening situation. The technology exists today that a baby born as early as 25 weeks has a halfway decent chance of surviving. But back in 1949, the year I was born, being two months premature was a matter of life or death. Consequently, I spent the first six weeks of my life in an incubator.

Although my parents loved me, a baby was the last thing they had time for. My mother was 39, Staff Director of the House Judiciary Committee, and a lawyer. My father was 42 and a plastic surgeon, just beginning his lucrative practice. They were only married for two years before my birth. My mother often told me how when I was born, the doctor held me up by my heels and announced, "The first woman Supreme Court Justice." How's that for high expectations? While Sandra Day O'Connor may have beaten me to that position, I proudly call myself the Supreme Court Jester.

As an adult looking back, I now realize how difficult it must have been for my parents to maintain their demanding careers while trying to raise a child. They both put in long hours at work so they could provide me with an enjoyable childhood. They wanted to give me everything, and they needed money to do that. So in order to help with the child raising and allow themselves to keep up with their hectic, full-time schedules, my parents hired a live-in housekeeper, Anne. Unfortunately, Anne was an alcoholic. One of my earliest recollections is of Anne holding me by my shoulders, yelling and shaking me. It was her way of punishing me for doing something wrong. I also remember watching her sneak liquor from my parents' liquor cabinet and then replacing the missing liquid with water. I quickly learned to keep my distance from her. That's why I was so happy when I was old enough to go to school. I thought it would be a respite from the chaos and pressure that housekeeper caused me at home. I was wrong.

I never thought there was anything funny about my last name (my maiden name) until I went to school. When the teacher called my name for attendance, "Jacki Dick," all my classmates began to chuckle. I couldn't figure out why…until I started hearing the jokes. My nickname quickly became "Dicki Jack" and my father was called "Dictor Doc" instead of Dr. Dick. I won't go into the more detailed jokes here (some of them can get vulgar), so I'll allow you to use your imagination. Let's just say that kids – even those as young as first grade – can be very cruel when you have an unusual or funny last name.

As if the name issue weren't enough, I also had the pleasure of being the shortest kid in the class. As an adult, I only stand four feet-ten inches (when my hair is clean), and I've grown quite a bit since childhood. So between my name and my height, I had more than my fair share of teasing. Add to that my alcoholic housekeeper and high profile parents, and it's a wonder I didn't have a nervous breakdown before age 10.

When children grow up with such stress, there are a number of ways they deal with it. Some kids become really quiet; others act out and get in trouble with the law. I decided to take a different route. I chose to deal with my situation by using my sense of humor. I became the class clown.

22

While I got a lot of laughs from my classmates, I also got in a lot of trouble from my teachers. I found a way to get the attention I didn't get from my parents. Cracking jokes and causing mass laughter soon became my specialty. As long as people were laughing, I reasoned, their attention was off me and all my perceived "short"comings (no pun intended). When fourth grade arrived, I began classes at National Cathedral School, which is a private Episcopalian girls' school. My fourth grade teacher had heard about my "clowning" escapades in grades K through third, and she revealed to me on the first day of school that she hoped I had "outgrown" that behavior and was now ready to act like a "young lady." No such luck.

Every morning at school we had chapel service and we had to line up by height. Since I was the shortest, I was always first in line. As usual, though, I'd have to crack a joke, tell a funny story, or do something else that inevitably led to a laughter casualty (those moments when you can't stop laughing uncontrollably). The teachers always knew I was the one responsible for the group laughter (no one else was brazen enough to evoke such merriment during a solemn service), so I'd be sent to the back of the chapel line as punishment. That meant I had to walk behind Courtie Worth – the tallest girl in the school and the center of the girls' basketball team. Being as short as I was, it was obvious that I had gotten in trouble and was being reprimanded.

In art class I would throw clay on the ceiling. I wasn't trying to be destructive; I just knew that the image of big gray blobs stuck to a ceiling made people laugh, so I did it. I'd get in trouble for that too. I don't think a day went by that I didn't carry a note home for my parents to sign.

While the laughter made me and everyone else feel good on the outside, it was only masking the pain I felt on the inside. I didn't feel good about who I was. I was the classic underachiever. I remember being enrolled in the remedial classes in school, which only added to my low self-esteem and self-worth. I felt that I could never measure up to anyone, especially my parents. I was a short, stocky child with the last name of "Dick," and my parents were these brilliant people whom I felt I could never please. My mother wrote half of the 1964 civil rights legislation when she was Staff Director of the House Judiciary Committee. My father was a dentist who decided he wanted to practice medicine. So he worked his way through medical school as a dentist and eventually specialized in plastic surgery. They were both successful in every sense of the word.

Years later I realized that in spite of all the negative emotions I harbored during my childhood, I had the uncanny ability to connect with people and establish lifelong friendships. In fact, I met my dear friend Babette when I was three years old, and I have other friends, Laurie, Stacey, Lynne, and Patti, whom I first met when I was nine. So I started thinking…what was it about me that enabled me to form such lasting relationships? I have to think it was my sense of humor. My humor is what let my spirit feel free and connect with others.

Before I go any further, let me clarify one point. I don't want people to think that my childhood was completely horrid. All throughout my childhood I got the message that my parents loved me; they just didn't know how to always express it. Perhaps they thought that providing me with all the material possessions I could want would be enough to show their love. I don't know for sure. They have since crossed to the other side, and I haven't asked them yet why they opted for a housekeeper rather than earn less money and be home with me. My best guess is that they each had their own agendas.

Fortunately, when I was ten years old, I developed the courage to confront my parents about the housekeeper and her drinking problem. I remember the day vividly. It was Saturday – a warm spring day. The sky outside was a deep azure blue. There was a slight breeze that calmed the sun's rays. I smelled rebirth in the air as the trees were starting to bloom and the first hint of plant life was peeking its head through the ground. I knew that would be the day to make my stand about the housekeeper.

I made my way down the stairs from my bedroom. My parents were in the kitchen drinking their morning coffee. I marched into the kitchen, stood in front of the table where they sat, put my hands on my hips and said, "Okay, one of us is leaving. It's either the housekeeper or me." And I was fully prepared to leave. In my mind I had the image of a cartoon me walking down the street carrying a stick on my shoulder. At the end of the stick was a kerchief that held all my worldly possessions. Venturing out into the world alone seemed like a better alternative than living at home and feeling so threatened.

I packed my belongings and left later that day.

Well, maybe not … actually, after that conversation my parents checked the liquor cabinet and realized that the liquor had indeed been watered down. They subsequently fired the housekeeper and employed a new one who was much more competent to take care of me. Their ability to believe me despite my record for causing trouble in school was a powerful lesson in the depth of their love for me.

Throughout my childhood, I did receive some wonderful, non-materialistic gifts from my parents. For example, my mother was a giggler like me, so I think I got my sense of humor from her. She was also a fearful person, though, so I must have gotten my courage from my father. The more I think about it, if it weren't for my father, I never would have had a swing set, I never would have learned how to play tennis, I never would have learned how to drive a car, I never would have gone to sporting events. So there were times of intense normalcy for me growing up…and love. Yes, there was lots of love. And my parents always told me, "Jacki, you can be anything you want to be in life." Unfortunately, I never knew what that was.

Even after high school and college, I still floundered professionally. I had gone through pre-med classes with the hopes of becoming a doctor one day. After graduating, I decided that medicine wasn't the path I wanted to take, so I decided to take the medical laboratory route instead. I spent a number of years working in medical laboratories wondering what I should do with my life.

By this time I was married to my husband Alex and starting a family, and I was completely content with my personal/ family life; however, my work life was a different story. I wasn't happy in my career and didn't know what to do. I lived my whole life watching my mother and father succeed in their prestigious careers, and I wanted so much to follow them and make them proud and claim my own sense of accomplishment.

When I was 34 and still unhappy in my career, tragedy struck. My mother died suddenly of a heart attack. I was devastated. Even though she was older and had been critically ill off and on since I was 10 years old, I thought her health was stable at the time, so her death shocked me and left me sad and bitter. I turned to my father for support, and he in turn came to me. While my mother's death was difficult for both my father and me, it somehow brought us closer than we had ever been. For the next ten years, my father and I bonded in a way we never had before. We talked about topics that would have been unheard of in the past – topics such as spirituality, our dreams, our hopes, and our opinions on controversial topics. For the first time in my life I looked at my father as not just my dad, but also as my friend. I cherished our dinners together and evenings at the Kennedy Center.

Because of these new conversations with my dad, he helped me realize that I wanted to spend my life helping people on a personal level. I decided that I should go into Social Work, and he encouraged me to pursue that goal. So I enrolled in graduate school to obtain my Master's degree. Four years later I graduated and embarked on my new career with an MSW (Master's of Social Work).

Four years after graduation, tragedy struck again. My father died of congestive heart failure. I was 44 years old. His death affected me more than my mother's – but in a strangely positive way. With both my parents gone, I felt for the first time that although an orphan, my spirit had the opportunity to soar. As I began looking back on my life and on my professional choices, I realized that I had been living my whole life based on what I believed their perception of me would be, so I never felt I could truly follow my heart and attain my life's mission. With them gone, however, I was able to finally let go of those childhood limitations and pursue my dreams. I've come to understand now that no matter what I would have done with my life would have been okay with them, but while they were alive, I was unable to accept that fact. It's a sad reality I wish I would have comprehended earlier.

The Path to Laughter

After obtaining my MSW degree, I somehow got on a mailing list of conferences and meetings. Every day my mailbox was filled with pamphlets, letters, brochures, and information packs about various conferences taking place around the world. They each promised to be "the one and only conference you'll ever need to further your career." I threw most of the mailings in the garbage either because they didn't interest me or because I didn't have the time. I was, after all, a busy wife and mother who also had a thriving psychotherapy practice. Leaving for a few days to attend a conference was the last thing on my to-do list.

There was one mailing that caught my attention, though. It was for an organization called The HUMOR Project in Saratoga Springs, New York. I learned from the pamphlet that it was a conference about humor and how it relates to health, education business, relationships, therapy, and a whole spectrum of topics. I was intrigued with the humor angle, especially given my childhood experiences with humor, so I put the pamphlet aside with the intention of getting more information.

Because of my work and family, I got busy with everyday life issues and never did look at that pamphlet again. Luckily, I received another one the next year. Again, I was intrigued, so I filed it for later review. Within a couple of weeks I forgot about it…again. But, as fate would have it, I received yet another mailing from The HUMOR Project the following year. This time I decided not to put the mailing aside but to act on it immediately. I enrolled for the conference in 1994, and in April of that year I made my trek up to New York to learn about humor. It was at that conference when I learned that my sense of humor was a gift – one that could be shared to help others. So that's when I started realizing that instead of being sent to the back of the chapel line for laughing, I could actually get paid for it and use humor in my career.

After that initial conference, I became enthralled with humor and healing and began learning all I could about the subject. I read books, attended more workshops, and talked with anyone who would discuss the topic with me. Six months after attending that first workshop, I jumped in with both feet and began conducting my own workshops about humor and health. I also used the humor concepts in my psychotherapy practice.

The workshops were a success, and people were readily accepting the humor and healing connection. Time and time again people would come up to me and say how they felt so much better – both physically and emotionally – after engaging in a good laugh. I knew I had taken another step towards my white light.

Two years into my new calling, I was invited to be a guest on a local radio show. The topic for discussion was Humor Therapy. Allen Klein, the world-renowned authority on the topic of humor and health, was the expert guest, and I was the "local yokel" who was adding the hometown flair. I brought my toilet bank with me to the studio. It's a small coin bank that resembles a toilet. In order to deposit your coins, you put them in the bowl and then "flush" them down the drain, at which time the bank then makes the sound of a toilet flushing. I thought such a prop would be good for a radio show, especially since the audio portion is so vivid.

During the course of the discussion, Allen Klein, who was joining the discussion via phone, got disconnected. As the producers tried to get him back on the line, I had to fill the airspace. Talk about stress! I had nowhere near the expertise of Allen Klein, yet here I was answering questions intended for him and interacting with the callers. To me, simply being a guest on the same show as Allen was an honor. I never dreamed I'd be the one to lead the discussion.

The producers finally got Allen back on the line and he took control of the questions and answers once again. When the spot ended, the show's host gave out the contact information for both Allen and me. I decided to write down Allen's e-mail address. I figured you never know when you might need it.

The following week I had an idea. Since I already had made contact with Allen and we had something in common professionally, why not take it a step further and ask him to be my mentor? I sent him an e-mail that day. In it, I told him how grateful I was to be on the show with him and how much I enjoyed hearing his views on the topic. I then included the all-important question: "As I expand my Humor Therapy practice, would you be my mentor?" As I hit the "send" button, I felt my pulse quicken. I wanted so much for him to say yes, but I also didn't want to get my hopes up. I knew he was a busy man and probably got multiple requests from people each day asking him to mentor them.

The next day I immediately checked my e-mail box. To my astonishment, there was a reply from Allen. I double-clicked on the message and read his response. He told me how he enjoyed being on the show as well and how he hoped he was able to help some people with his words. He then answered my mentoring question. He said yes! I was ecstatic.

From that day on, Allen and I have communicated about various professional decisions I had to make. Throughout it all, Allen gave me constant encouragement and the will to keep going. I believe that he is one of my angels, for without his support and advice through the years, I may very well just have given up.

Spiritual Patchwork

In 1998, the movie *Patch Adams* hit the theatres. Since it was about a doctor who believed in the value of humor and healing, I, of course, wanted to see it. So my husband and I, along with two of our best friends, went to the theatre one evening to see the movie. While my husband and friends kept a dry eye from beginning to end, I cried throughout the entire movie. After the movie ended, I cried till I shook. I felt its impact on a visceral level. The work the movie depicted, and the struggle Patch had to go through to attain it, moved me. It stirred a kind of connection deep within my soul. Before I rose from my seat to leave the theatre that night, I knew my true calling in life: I was going to focus my life on humor and healthcare. I was determined to bring my humor into any healthcare facility that would have me. The next day, with my eyes still full of tears, I picked up the phone, called the hospital closest to my home, and asked to speak to someone in volunteer services. When I got a lady on the phone, I immediately said, "My name is Jacki Kwan. I'm a Humor Consultant, and I want to offer my services to your hospital."

The moment I uttered the words, I felt a new sense of peace overcome my body. I knew immediately that I was doing the right thing. The hospital representative and I spoke for a while, and then she told me that she'd bring the issue to the hospital committee and call me back. A few days later I received a phone call stating that the committee said yes to my offer. So, in January 1999, I officially started my new life's mission of being a Humor Therapist.

Prior to my first day at the hospital, I envisioned my work there as being similar to the *Patch Adams* movie. I saw myself going around from room to room, offering good humor to those who needed me most. But things didn't turn out quite like that. I showed up my first day right on time. As I walked through the front door and made my way down the hall to the volunteer office, I noticed people staring and giggling at me. I couldn't figure out why. After all, what could be all that funny about a four foot-ten inch woman wearing a volunteer jacket and a big purple hat – kind of like a hat you'd see in the Dr. Seuss book *A Cat in a Hat*. Sure, I had humorous buttons pinned all over my volunteer jacket, was carrying an array of silly props, and wore teabags as earrings, but was that so unusual? I guess it was.

After checking in with the volunteer office and explaining my get-up, I was ready for my first assignment. *Where would they want me,* I wondered. *The oncology unit? The critical care wing? The general floors?* Nope. They put me in Pediatrics. They felt a "clown" would be better accepted there than any other wing. Did I mind? No way! I was doing what I loved and touching the lives of children in need. Besides, I figured that once they saw what I did and gained some trust in me, they'd turn me loose in the rest of the hospital.

I was right! Two months later I had gained the trust of many in the hospital and was authorized to visit units other than Pediatrics. The more people I interacted with, the more I knew this was my true calling in life. My spirit felt so free yet so connected with each and every person. I knew I had to take my Humor Therapy a step further, so I made an important decision that changed my career forever.

A Fateful Meeting

At the time, I knew another Humor Project conference was scheduled for April 1999, and I also knew that many of the people I had previously met there the year before would be attending. I was especially interested in visiting one nurse in the area, Leslie Gibson, because she had been doing humor programs in hospitals for over ten years. I called her prior to attending the conference and asked if I could spend a few days with her after the conference to learn first-hand how she ran her Humor Therapy program so successfully. She agreed.

During the course of my visit with Leslie, she mentioned to me that the following month (May) she would be sponsoring

Dr. Kataria to come from India. I had originally heard of Dr. Kataria two years earlier. He wrote the book *Laugh For No Reason* and is the founder of Laughter Clubs where groups of people come together for therapeutic laughing sessions. When I first heard of Laughter Clubs, I thought they were an amazing idea, but I was never able to get enough information to pursue the topic further. Now I was getting my chance to not only learn about the clubs, but also to meet the man who founded them. I was ecstatic. I told Leslie I would definitely visit her in May.

So May finally came and I was scheduled on a nonstop flight leaving from Dulles airport and arriving in Tampa, Florida. Although I packed my bags the night before, I was still running late. My flight was scheduled to leave at 10 a.m., and I just arrived at the airport at 9:15 a.m. That gave me only 45 minutes to check-in, locate my gate, and board. I was convinced I'd never make it.

After checking-in at the counter I made my way to the security check point. At this point I only had 15 minutes until my flight left. As I approached the security gate, I noticed there were four lines open. At the entrance of each line stood a menacing-looking guard. I got in what looked like the shortest line and checked my watch. Thirteen minutes till take off.

Finally, my turn came at the checkpoint. I placed all my carry-on items on the conveyer belt: my purse, my small overnight bag, and the gift I was bringing to Leslie – a comical walking cane that came fully-equipped with a rearview mirror and honking horn. Upon seeing the walking cane, every stern-looking guard cracked a smile. One even came over to me and asked to see the cane. At first he was following protocol by checking the cane for drugs or other illegal items, but then he began having fun with it. He pretended to use the cane and honked the horn, which consequently made the other guards want to play with it too. Soon every guard at that post was hysterical laughing and playing with the silly cane. Although I was scared I was going to miss my flight, my spirit was soaring as I saw these seriously overworked individuals have a little fun.

After some prompting from me, they returned the cane and I made my mad dash to my gate. I made a sharp right turn around one corner and bumped into the tallest man I had ever seen. To me, he looked as if he were twelve feet tall. He was wearing clothes that didn't match. His long gray hair had a blue streak down one side, and he wore a square hat. I looked at him for a moment and a surge of recollection triggered in my brain. I had seen this man before. Then it hit me.

"Are you Patch A-a-a-a-dams?" I stammered.

"Yes," he replied.

Then we shared a moment of silence. In that moment, our eyes connected and I felt his spirit, his energy, so deeply.

At that point I wanted the funniest words that had ever crossed human lips to come from my mouth, but all I could manage was an intelligent sounding "bl-bl-bl-bl-bl-bl-bl." It was as if my index finger was stuck flipping my bottom lip up and down.

Then Patch saved me from humiliating myself further and said to me, "Now that you've introduced me to me, who are you?"

I went on to tell him my name and where I was going. As it turned out, Patch knew Leslie too, as well as Dr. Kataria. In fact, we had a number of mutual acquaintances. We made some additional small talk, and as much as I hated to, I had to say good-bye to Patch. My plane was due to leave in less than five minutes and I still had to get to the gate. So we said our farewells and I dashed off to my flight.

I sat on the plane thinking about the course of events and how wonderfully fateful it was that I ran into Patch Adams. I wondered if I'd ever see him again. A feeling deep down inside me said that I would.

On the Road Again

Upon returning from Florida, my spirit was soaring. Not only did I learn more about Humor Therapy and new ways to incorporate it into healthcare settings, but I also met two of my professional heroes: Dr. Kataria and Patch Adams. I also met an incredible individual named Steve Wilson, who is the co-creator of the World Laughter Tour along with Karyn Buxman. Steve gave me my initial exposure to the concept of a Laughter Club. He also gave me a precious gift no one had ever given before: a boost of self-confidence. Steve saw incredible potential in me, and he wasn't shy about telling me exactly what he thought. In fact, Steve was so confident in my abilities that he asked me to be on the Board of Directors for the World Laughter Tour. Of course I said yes!

Armed with this overwhelming sense of inspiration, I expanded my Humor Therapy program at the hospital and created HA!HA!LOGY®, which is a facility-wide Therapeutic Humor program designed to enhance the emotional, physical, and spiritual health of patients. I ran the HA!HA!LOGY department for the following six months, and then something wonderful happened.

By now it was November 1999. After arriving home from work one evening, I checked the pile of mail that was on the kitchen table. Among all the bills and junk there was a letter addressed to me. I didn't recognize the handwriting, and when I read the return address, I gasped. There, in my hands, was a personal letter from none other than Patch Adams. I tore the envelope open as fast and as carefully as I could. I wanted to read immediately what Patch had to say, yet I didn't want to ruin the envelope. To me, it was a precious gift that should be treasured – a reassurance that the moment was indeed true.

In the letter was a personal invitation from Patch for me to join him on a trip to China with 44 other clowns to spread laughter throughout Chinese hospitals, nursing homes, orphanages, hostels, and anywhere else there were people who needed humor. After reading the letter, my initial response was, "Oh my God!!!!!" I couldn't believe that of all the people Patch knew and had recently met that he would invite me to join his group. I was ecstatic…and I was scared. After all, what did I know about being a professional clown? Sure, I dressed silly and acted funny when I was doing HA!HA!LOGY sessions; however, traveling with a group of professional clowns was another story. I immediately began calling everyone I knew to get their opinion on what I should do. Some people told me stories of how emotionally draining Patch's Russian trip was the year before, while other people explained that this was a once in a lifetime opportunity. I decided I needed a few weeks to think about it. The trip wasn't until September 2000, and the letter said that I needed to have my response in by February 2000.

During my "thinking it over" time, my attention got distracted. I was so excited about the possibility of going to China that I was filled with an unending enthusiasm to talk about it with whomever would listen. A few days after receiving the letter from Patch, I was speaking with a friend, Sandy Guritzky, who is one of my regular tennis partners at the country club we both belong to. Sandy is also on the Board of Directors of the Hebrew Home of Greater Washington. I've always respected and admired Sandy, and talking with him was always a joy.

Sandy was familiar with my work at the local hospital as a Humor Therapist. He was always interested in what I was doing to help ease the patients. The news of my possible trip to China seemed to have a profound impact on him. He asked question after question. He was enthralled with the idea of traveling to a foreign country halfway around the world to spread joy and happiness to young and old alike. He told me that he was going to mention me and my work to the CEO of the Hebrew Home to see if a Humor Therapy program could be started there.

A couple of weeks later I received a phone call from Cheryl Brown, the Director of Activities at the Hebrew Home. She asked if I would be interested in meeting with her to discuss whether or not my HA!HA!LOGY program would be a good fit for their organization. I immediately said yes.

Two days later I was sitting in her office. We talked about Humor Therapy and the many health benefits of laughing. I showed her my various props and funny hats and told her about my invitation to go to China. She seemed excited about the idea of implementing a Humor Therapy program in the Hebrew Home. I left the meeting that day with a sense of excitement and accomplishment. I knew I was on my way to spreading my ideas of Humor Therapy beyond the walls of the local hospital.

I expected to get some kind of feedback from the Hebrew Home within a week. When two weeks came and went with no word from anyone, I started to get worried. Maybe she didn't like the idea of Humor Therapy after all, I thought. Maybe she thought they could spend their money more wisely elsewhere. Or even worse, maybe she simply didn't like me. I let my imagination get the best of me and think the worst. Three weeks later I called Cheryl, only to learn that she was still going over their budget and thinking about her options. She told me she'd call when they were ready to proceed.

By late December 1999 I still hadn't heard back from anyone at the Hebrew Home, so I concluded that they had decided against a Humor Therapy program. The following month, however, Cheryl called me with some fantastic news.

A donor in the community had given a substantial amount of money to the Hebrew Home. As a result of that generous donation, HA!HA!LOGY had a new home at the Home. I could barely believe my ears or contain my excitement. Because of my childhood ties to the Hebrew Home, I was certainly thrilled about working there.

On February 1, 2000, I officially began my work at the Hebrew Home. I continued working at the hospital and alternated the days in which I visited each location. As I walked through the front doors of the Hebrew Home that day and made my way down the hall to the activities office, I felt a new sense of pride and accomplishment. For the first time, I could sense the spirit of my grandmother, who died at the Hebrew Home over 40 years ago, and the spirits of both my parents cheering me on. Deep down I knew they were all proud of me and that they supported me in my decision to spread humor and joy to all.

Walking around the Home that day gave me a new connection to my past as well as my future. As I interacted with the staff and residents, I felt a new spiritual peace overtake my body. I was in a place where I could embrace my Jewish upbringing of the past while reaching out to form new future relationships that could nourish my soul. The little voice inside me said that I was exactly where I should be. I was "home," and it felt absolutely wonderful.

A Clown is Hatched

Now that it was February, I had to give my response regarding the China trip. Because my Humor Therapy program was now in two local healthcare settings, I had a newfound confidence that I could handle the emotional sacrifice such a trip would entail. When I finally called in my RSVP, however, the lady coordinating the trip informed me that it was full. My heart sank. I asked if she could put my name on a cancellation list, and she did. So at this point I had no idea whether or not I was going to go.

When I told my professional colleagues about my China trip decision and the outcome, they immediately started telling me about Clown Camp. "If there's a chance you're going to go to China, you'll have to go dressed as a clown," they all said. And they were right. When I called about the China trip to check my waiting list status, the person I spoke to confirmed that dressing as a clown was a requirement. So, even though I still didn't know whether I was going to China or not, I decided to enroll in Clown Camp.

The next Clown Camp session began May 18, 2000 in La Crosse, Wisconsin. The day before I left for camp, I received a phone call from Patch's office. Someone had cancelled for the China trip, so I was in. Talk about timing! I was so excited, and knowing that China was in my future made Clown Camp even more of a life changing experience.

Looking back now, it's amazing how profound an impact the camp had on my spirit. During that fateful week in La Crosse, my clown character "Elfinya" was hatched. As I peeked out of my shell that week and began to waddle around in my new persona, an amazing spiritual evolution started to unfold.

Before I went to Clown Camp, I was really into the funny, silly, ha-ha part of clowning. Clown camp taught me that there are different types of clowns, and the kind of clown I wanted to be was a "caring clown," as these are the kind of clowns that work in healthcare settings.

The first day of camp I learned there was going to be a clown makeup artist named Jim Howle there who was once a makeup artist at Ringling Brothers. I asked him to help me design my clown face. I had no idea what to expect from Jim, but the makeup image I had in my mind looked something like the Mimi character from the Drew Carey Show. I envisioned myself with the big, flippy hair and bright blue tacky makeup. I wasn't yet connected to the softer side of clowning, so a harsh face seemed appropriate to me.

Before beginning the makeup, Jim asked me to explain what I did for a living. I told him that I work in healthcare with all sorts of patients, from those in intensive care and the cancer ward to pediatrics and postoperative recovery. Upon hearing that, Jim worked his magic. He designed for me a much softer clown face with lavender eye shadow and a straight lavender wig.

When I first saw my new clown face, my heart softened. "This is it!" I thought. The change in makeup became a metaphor for the softening of my clown character. Before clown camp, my shtick was funny, but my funniness had an edge. The before-camp (B.C.) image of myself that comes to mind is that of a half circle, kind of like the letter "D." At the top and bottom of the letter D there are points – sharp corners. That sharpness related to the interactions I was having with patients, as the funniness was still silly and crazy. After Jim suggested this softer look, the corners of my "D" softened too. He helped me give voice to the spirit of laughter, enabling the corners of my "D" to come together to make a circle. So after clown camp, I felt like the spiritual piece of my clowning was filled out, and this gave me a whole new definition of the phrase "clowning around" (a-round).

The realization of my clown name, "Elfinya," also carries great significance. It's derived from my computer name "elf in self." At my very first humor conference I attended a lecture given by Joel Goodman on basic humor concepts. During that lecture, he mentioned that if you look at the word "self" you'd notice it contains the word "elf." As we all know, elves are humorous, little, fictitious creatures who are carefree and don't take themselves too seriously. They like to have fun and to laugh. Joel emphasized the point that we all need to find that "elf" in ourselves, and for those words of wisdom, I'm forever grateful. I think at Clown Camp I really did discover the little elf-like creature that is within – I discovered Elfinya. And I want to share that part of myself with everyone I meet.

A New Me

The first day after I was back home from Clown Camp I went to the hospital. I arrived in my full clown costume and makeup and was amazed at the difference it made to be there as a clown as opposed to me with just props and hats. I received much more non-verbal feedback and smiles from not just the kids, but also from the adults. I realized that kids will fill in the blanks – figuratively, that is. For example, Before Elfinya (B.E.), as I walked down the halls, the kids would say to their parents, "Look at the clown!" I only had on my volunteer jacket with funny buttons on it, a wild hat, and my tea bag earrings, yet the kids still related to me as a clown. Now as Elfinya, the adults joined in with the kids' excitement, making me even gladder that Elfinya had hatched.

Once in a while B.E., an adult visitor would ask me to visit their friend or family member in room such and such. That first day as Elfinya, however, at least five adults asked me to please visit someone! Being Elfinya made a huge difference. She gave a wonderful softness that was missing from just plain "me."

The most profound experience my first week back occurred at the Hebrew Home while I was conducing a stress management workshop for the staff. I had wanted to go to the Alzheimer's unit to put my new training into practice, but I had to set up my props and overheads for the staff's seminar. I was a little disappointed because I wanted to spend as much time as possible with the residents. While I was setting up, though, I noticed that in the back of the room was a resident in a wheelchair with her husband standing beside her. The resident wasn't speaking, and she and her husband were hovering around the fish tank.

I started to approach them. As I got closer, I could tell the woman was severely mentally compromised, so I down shifted into my slowest gear. At this point there were 40-50 people in the room waiting for me to begin my seminar, but I didn't care. I was drawn to this woman. So I, or rather Elfinya, continued to approach her.

I got within 10 feet or so of her, and then I stopped. She looked up and saw me. I took a few more steps towards her. She looked at me hesitantly. I took two steps backwards. Slowly, she extended her hand to me. I s-l-o-w-l-y approached her and took her hand. Her eyes began to sparkle, so mine did too. She then began to look a little frightened, so I took another small step back. That made her feel more comfortable, and she took her other hand and placed it on mine. I then slowly took a nearby chair with my free hand and ever so gently pulled it close to her so I could mirror her posture, which was seated. At this point the room was very quiet as people looked on. Suddenly, the magic began!

She started making some sounds – some undecipherable words – and I followed her lead. Together, we "sang." She couldn't speak words, and it didn't matter. As she "spoke," her cheeks danced. I followed her lead. I paced my breath with hers and "sang" in the same tones that she did. Her sounds continued…and then she started to laugh! Can you imagine? She laughed and I laughed with her. I felt like I was giggling with angels.

Then she slowly took one of her hands off of mine and reached out to cup my cheek in it. At that very nanosecond, as if we had rehearsed it, we both exhaled together in perfect synchrony. For that brief moment, our spirits connected. Her brain may have been compromised, but her spirit was very much alive. As I looked up at the people around me, there wasn't a dry eye in the room. I never felt so much gratitude for Elfinya as I did at that moment. I knew I had a gift. I could speak "clown" and I could connect with others on a very personal and spiritual level. From that day on, I could hardly wait to get to China so I could share my unique gift.

Chinese Patchwork

For the next four months I roamed the halls of the hospital and the Hebrew Home as my new Elfinya, constantly counting the days until I'd go to China with Patch and the other 44 clowns. When the trip finally arrived, I was a bundle of nerves. I arrived at the hotel meeting room that afternoon two hours early so I could meet my fellow clown companions. As each person arrived and we introduced ourselves to each other, the chatter and the laughter became louder and louder.

We then boarded a bus for the airport and the incessant talking and giggling continued. When we entered the airport terminal, it was like a rush of uncontrollable energy swooshed through the automatic doors. Everyone in the terminal turned their heads to witness this phenomenon of 45 people filled with excitement storming the grounds. I think we lifted the entire mood of the airport terminal when we arrived, and even more so when we left, as our absence made the sound decibel level plummet.

The plane ride to China was our last chance for relaxation. From the moment we disembarked we were in a constant state of motion – always visiting just one more unit, interacting with just one more patient, staying up just one more hour to reveal the joyous events of the day with our fellow clowns. We were clowning for 12-14 hours a day in hospitals, nursing homes, orphanages, and in public places, engaging with all different kinds of people and interacting in a variety of situations.

While in China, I had the opportunity to be a part of one profound incident that will forever stick in my mind and that reaffirmed to me that I'm using my gifts the way my spirit was destined to. We were in the children's hospital, interacting with various patients and their families. Some of my fellow clowns had begun "clowning" with patients, and I knew not to interrupt them or join in – I had to find my own people to interact with. One of the main rules of clowning is that if you see another clown begin to interact with someone, you're supposed to simply let them be. You don't join in unless the other clown specifically asks you to do so.

So as each of my clown mates picked a room to enter, I continued walking down the hospital's dark, musty corridor. After a few moments, I walked past the doorway to an examining room. Inside was a very little girl, probably two or three years old, sitting with her mother. They were waiting for a doctor to come in and see them. I don't remember seeing a door for this particular examining room, so the doorway was completely open and there was a window in addition to the doorway that allowed me to see inside the examining room.

Something about this little girl called to me. My entire spirit wanted to interact with her. I approached her very cautiously because many people are afraid of clowns – even adults. I could tell by looking at the girl that she was scared. Even so, that little voice inside me said to interact with this little person. So I stood about three feet outside the doorway and looked at her. Our eyes made contact, and she looked shyly away. I just stayed where I was and continued watching her. She looked at me again, and then she looked away.

The next time she looked at me, I put my head down, looked at her from the corner of my eye, and acted as if I were shy. She did the same. We played this little game for a while, the whole time with her clinging to her mom's shoulders.

I then walked very slowly over to the window that looked into her examining room and played the "I look at you, you look at me" game with her through the window. After doing that for a few moments, I began to peek around the door, almost like a like a peek-a-boo game. At that point, she smiled, and I knew I was beginning to engage her. So I took a step to be right in the doorway, and then I stopped. I let her reaction be my cue as to how to proceed. I'd take a step into the room, watch her expression, and then either stop or take a step backwards. This interaction went on for about twenty-five minutes.

Finally I got completely into the room, and the girl's mom sat her down in her lap. There was a little child's chair in the room, so I pulled that chair close to them and sat in it. I love those little kids' chairs. They're the only chairs I can sit in where my feet don't swing underneath. As I sat there with them, I began to blow some bubbles. The little girl loved the bubbles. She put her hands out to catch the soapy orbs, giggling the whole time. When I stopped blowing the bubbles, the little girl climbed down from her mother's lap and gave me a great big hug. I was completely blown away! My spirit was soaring to new heights.

I was so touched that I felt the tears welling up in my eyes. I didn't want to cry in front of the girl, so I got up, blew her a kiss, and made my way out the door. At that point the reality of the situation hit me. Here we were in this dingy, hot, musty hospital where care standards are so far below what we're used to in America. There was no air conditioning, and I was drenched in sweat. Yet, despite these physical obstacles, I was able to come in, and without saying a word, I made someone relax and laugh. That awesome experience is what it's all about.

So I walked out of the room and down the hall. When I turned around to look back at where I came from, I saw the mom and the girl outside in the hallway playing with 10-15 other clowns. I was so engrossed by my own interaction with the girl that I didn't even notice there were other clowns outside the door watching.

Going to China was truly a growth experience for me. It was an opportunity for me to take some risks and follow my gut. What was truly wondrous was watching all these other clowns do their thing, because not all of them worked in healthcare. Some of them were birthday party clowns while others were circus clowns. Seeing the different ways they interacted gave me a chance to learn new approaches and new ways to connect with others.

I also learned that the sound of laughter has no accent. That's right. The words "Ha-Ha" translate into Chinese. Although we had an interpreter with us, we didn't need his services during the laughter or hugs portion of our visits. Humor Therapy transcends ethnicities and cultural barriers, so it doesn't matter if you and the person you're interacting with don't speak the same language. Humor is spiritual, and everyone can connect on a spiritual level.

What became crystal clear in my mind as a result of venturing to China is that people's brains and bodies may be compromised by an illness, but their spirits are very much alive. There's something about a Therapeutic Clown that can elicit that spirit. For example, one day we went to Beijing Songtang Hospital. It was a primitive facility – dirty, almost open air, with a stench of urine. The rooms were dark, dank, and barren. I wandered by myself into the room of an old man who was sitting in a chair beside his bed. He looked tall, very skinny, and he was wearing old, torn pajamas.

I approached him quietly, and at first I just looked into his eyes and smiled. He smiled too. When I extended my hands to him, he took them and held them. I couldn't connect through words with him because the words we each used were very different, so I decided to see if he would follow me in some quiet giggling. I started with a gleam in my eye. He followed. I paced my breath with his. He continued to smile with his eyes. I started a quiet giggle. His face lit up. He smiled with his whole body even though he seemed very weak. He had a grin from ear to ear, proudly showing the few rotted teeth that were left in his mouth. He didn't want to stop smiling or let me go. What a blessing to share that moment with a sick and dying man. After that day I knew I would never doubt the value or power of laughter again. I have a huge mission to spread as much joy throughout the universe as I can. People desperately need it and want it, and I desire nothing more than to fulfill those wishes.

Clowning Around in the Streets of China

We spent a total of 10 days in China. On the last day, I decided it was time to let loose, have some fun, and take a few risks. We were in Shanghai at the People's Park, which is a huge grassy area with a wide sidewalk that has vendors and stores on each side. Some of the other clowns and I were walking down the street in our clown get-ups, and people were turning their heads and looking at us. I was in a very playful mood and decided to act on it.

To my left I saw some toy horses that little kids ride – the kind where you put a coin in and the horse goes round and round. I hopped on one of the horses, deposited my money, and commenced riding my horse like a Wild West Cowgirl. Chinese adults don't make a habit of playing on children's toys, so they were enthralled with my antics. Soon a crowed gathered around, and they happily watched me have one of the best times of my life. Watching them smile and laugh at me made me feel wonderful. Just then the store owner came out and asked me to leave. I was so upset, but I obliged. In trouble again!!!!

My clown friends and I continued walking down the sidewalk when I began to feel the pounding reverberations of live rock music playing. It felt as if life was being drummed into me. This definitely caught my attention, because when I was growing up I spent a lot of time alone listening to music in order to escape the chaos. Rock and roll music, Mo-Town, virtually any kind of popular music always got me going. I would sing and dance around the house for hours. So now, anytime I hear music, I'm just drawn to it.

As we walked a little further, the music got louder. So I said to my clown friends, "Let's go. Let's find out where this is coming from." We continued to walk and we came upon a stage area. There was a rope that matched the dimension of the stage and enclosed an area where there were about a hundred people or so sitting. On the outside of the rope area there was a crowd of people, about five deep, standing around this rope and watching these adorable, young, Chinese girls doing perfectly choreographed rock and roll style dance.

So I stood there watching the girls and I was rocking and rolling to the music. Being as small as I am, I was soon able to worm my way up to the rope's edge. While there, I began to imitate as best as I could the movements the girls were doing. One of the girls on stage saw me dancing and signaled for me to come up on stage. My immediate thought was, "No way!" But then I thought, "What the hell!" I decided that this would be my chance to cause a mass-scale laughter epidemic, so I went up on stage with the girls.

Remember now that I had my clown costume on and my full clown makeup. My clown suit was designed so that it had snaps around the crotch area, kind of like the way baby clothes do. As I climbed up on stage, I felt the snaps of my costume legs come undone. I tried to resnap them once I got up there, but my hands were shaking from nerves so much that I couldn't grasp the snaps correctly. I gave up trying to snap my pants shut and decided to go with the flow. I was a couple of steps behind what the girls were doing, and the crowd was hysterical. The more I heard them laugh, the freer I felt.

At the end of the dance routine, the girls fell down on the floor to their knees, collapsed their bodies onto their thighs, stretched one arm in front of them and tucked the other arm down by their side. It reminded me of the child's pose in yoga. By the time I ended the dance and fell on the stage floor, the audience was howling with laughter. I never felt so free in my life before. My spirit was up there rockin' and rollin'.

As soon as I walked off the stage I began looking for a private place where I could resnap the crotch in my pants. Lord only knows what the audience saw with me dancing at that point. But I really didn't care. I was just in the moment and having fun. Then a Chinese woman came running after me, tapped me on the shoulder, and gave me a present for dancing. It was a small basket with food and candies. That simple gesture touched my soul and made me realize once again just how intimately connected we all really are. I savored that moment for as long as I could.

That night as I lay in bed, I thought about my days in China, what I learned, and what I hoped to bring home with me. My days in China enabled my spirit to get closer to "home" than I ever imagined possible.

Chapter Three

The Halls are Alive with the Sound of Laughter

"Humor, more than anything else in the human makeup, affords an aloofness and an ability to rise above any situation, even if only for a few seconds."
– Victor Frankl

Traveling to China gave me a new appreciation for Therapeutic Humor. Upon returning home, I realized that when most people think of the word "humor," they think of jokes, pranks, silly antics…basically anything that can evoke a chuckle or a good hearty laugh. What they fail to realize is that even though those jokes and pranks are initiating laughter, they're sometimes doing so at the sake of someone's feelings. When this happens, the humor can have a negative effect and ultimately make a person feel depressed and unmotivated. This kind of negative humor is the furthest thing from the true essence of Humor Therapy.

In reality, laughter is only a part of the concept of humor. And sometimes, laughter isn't involved at all. When I talk about Therapeutic Humor, I'm referring to the act of getting someone into a more positive state of mind. How that process actually occurs depends on the person's physical and mental state and on what they physically and spiritually need at that moment in time. For example, when I work with people who are dying or who have mid to late stage Alzheimer's or Dementia, sometimes those people just need someone to sit and hold their hand and breathe with them. Because of their mental state, they don't comprehend jokes or silly faces or whoopee cushions. Such blatant slapstick humor as that would defeat the whole purpose and put them in a negative state of mind. You can't force someone to laugh; you can only give them what they're willing to receive. As humor scholar Harvey Mindess said, "You don't have to teach people to be funny; you just have to give them permission."

Humor Therapy is about giving people what they need at a particular point in time in order to be in a positive state of mind. It involves building rapport with a person and letting the other person know that you understand and, most important, that you care. During a Humor Therapy session, I do subtle things to connect with people on a spiritual level. I pace my breath with the other person. I mirror their gestures and movements so that we're in sync. And if the other person is making unintelligible sounds, as older people who are in late stages of Dementia or Alzheimer's often do, I "sing" along with them. The other person can then see, hear, and feel me on their level and form a connection. While the other person may not laugh or giggle, I often see the corners of their eyes begin to crinkle and the corners of their mouth lift. I notice that "spark" return to their face. As their cheeks fill with color, I feel as if I'm watching a Morning Glory open its petals in the early dawn light. When those moments occur, they're absolutely miraculous.

At the Hebrew Home, such marvelous events unfold before me daily. It happens when a depressed resident rolls by me in a wheelchair and nods to me in recognition. I feel the connection in an elderly woman's touch as she places her hand on mine. It's in the eyes of the elderly gentleman as he begs me to sit with him just one minute more. It's all these seemingly miniscule details that occur daily and that impact their lives – and mine – so profoundly.

My Personal Experience with Good Humor
(other than ice cream)

I mentioned earlier that as a child I used humor to help me deal with stress. As an adult, this still holds true. Let me give you a recent example of what I needed to be in good humor in order to get through a stressful situation.

A few years before my father died, he was diagnosed with colon cancer and went through surgery to remove polyps. Since your risk of certain cancers is hereditary, I decided I should have a colonscopy in 1999. This meant I'd have to go under anesthesia again, and after my whole surgical episode with my ovarian cyst, anesthesia was the last thing I wanted. I was terrified, to say the least. I needed a way to stay in good humor before the procedure, so I figured it was time for me to put my money where my mouth was.

I thought long and hard about what would put me in good humor in spite of my situation. It finally occurred to me…I needed a way to make others laugh right before they put me under the anesthesia. Hearing others laugh always puts me in a positive frame of mind, and if the sound of laughter could be the last thing I heard right before falling asleep, I knew I could keep my spirit up.

The night before my colonscopy I went to the drug store and bought some large adhesive bandages – the kind you put on skinned knees. On those bandages I wrote some little messages for the operating room staff. The next morning I placed the bandages on my derriere, so that when the staff opened my gown they'd have some humorous messages to read and laugh about.

I used five bandages in all to cover my bottom (I guess my butt's not that big after all). On one I drew a little picture of myself that has now become my signature piece. It's a little smiley face, and at the top there's a little sprig of hair coming up with a bow around it, kind of like Pebbles Flintstone. To the side of the picture I wrote, "Smile! We're on Candid Camera." Another bandage bore the phrase, "Shitless in Falls Church." (Falls Church is the name of the town where I had the procedure done, and to do a colonoscopy, you have to be "empty," if you know what I mean.) On the third one I wrote "Up ~~Yo~~ Mine." Another said, "Scared Shitless." The final one touts the phrase, "'N Stync."

Needless to say, when the staff pulled my gown open, the room burst into laughter. The timing couldn't have been more perfect. At that point I was just on the verge of feeling the full effects of the anesthesia, so the last thing I heard as I drifted off to sleep was the sweet sound of laughter. I felt totally relaxed and at peace, and that was precisely what I needed at that point in time.

The Connection Factor

Creating a spiritual connection with others is all about balance – being able to counter the funny with the serious. It's about helping someone by generating energy in the space between me and the other person. If I have a relationship with someone, the spiritual healing is "in the air" between us. The energy fills the space between me *and* the people I work with. The magic is in that *and* – between the person *and* me.

This energy is healing – or potentially healing, as we don't have scientific data on it yet. Regardless, this energy gives me a connection with people that often transcends life itself. Although I'm frequently very saddened when I hear that one of the residents has passed on, I am aware of the balance between sadness and missing that person and knowing that my life is a little bit richer because I had the opportunity to interact with them. As a result, I'm able to balance out a lot of different feelings that go along with both life and death.

Because of the spiritual connection I was able to create with them while they were living, I know that I can now call upon their energy around me even though they're no longer in the body they once were in, and I find that very comforting. The more I think of the spiritual connections I've been able to create with people as a result of Humor Therapy, the more I wonder if it's a spiritual signal when the person's memory suddenly pops into my head. I wonder if it's their way of connecting with me from "home." I think it is, and the greater balance I create in my life – of being able to counter the serious with the funny – the more in tune I become with the spiritual nature we all have within.

I searched long and hard for a way to represent that balance in pictorial form. At the beginning of each chapter, you'll notice a stick figure drawing of what appears to be a dancing person. A birthday present my daughter Jenifer gave me inspired that picture. The gift was a candleholder in the shape of the stick figure, with each hand balancing a large pillar candle. As soon as I saw it, I knew it was the perfect graphic to convey my message of balance and whimsy.

It shows the funny aspect of what I do (as indicated by the dancing cartooniness of the graphic), and it conveys the serious nature that permeates every aspect of my work (as indicated by the balanced hands). Receiving this gift was like a calling to my spirit, because when I first started doing Humor Therapy I felt as if I was out of balance. I primarily connected with the funny, silly, in your face kind of humor. Now I know, however, that there's so much more to humor. My graphic illustrates my "rounding out," my softening, as I am connecting with my spiritual self and learning how to deepen my connections with others.

That graphic also connected me with following my passion and creating my Humor Therapy program based on my personality. I like the feeling of movement and flexibility the figure portrays, because I incorporate dancing and singing into my Humor Therapy sessions whenever possible. I use that movement as a way to connect with others. I also know that I must have emotional and behavioral flexibility in my interactions in order to establish rapport. There's nothing worse that being silly with someone who is sad. I must accommodate whatever mood people are in when I greet them.

From my training in hypnosis and Neuro-Linguistic Programming (NLP), I've learned that if you change your body physiology, that is, the physical position of your body, you can change your emotional mindset. As I learned from Steve Wilson, if you throw your hands up in the air and smile, it's really hard to shout, "I'm depressed!" and mean it. That's why I use literally uplifting movements like that to help people discover what it means to be in good humor.

Through the use of NLP, I'm able to help people shift from a negative state of mind to a more positive one. I also use specific NLP rapport building techniques to better connect with others and to invite them into the present moment. These techniques involve mirroring someone's posture, gestures, tilt of the head, and sparkle in the eye. I mirror the sub-modalities of their voice, pitch, tone, and pace of speech. I do whatever I can to be in sync with the other person. When done successfully, I can connect with the other person so that we're on the same wavelength. The energy we then create together does wonders for the person's emotional being. It puts us in sync with each other, which requires a certain degree of flexibility.

I want to make it clear that during this process I never force anyone to participate in a Humor Therapy session if he or she doesn't want to. I recall one incident where I went to the Hebrew Home dressed as Elfinya. As I walked around and interacted with the various residents, one lady looked at me and said with her Russian accent, "What, are you crazy or something? How could anyone laugh? What's there to laugh at?"

I responded, "Yes. Laughing can seem crazy at times." And then I backed away from her. One of the greatest challenges for me is allowing people to have their own space when they really don't want to interact. I know in my head and in my actions that I give them that space they need, although it's difficult for me to accept the fact that some people would rather stay sour. I realize, however, that those people are where they need to be emotionally. And for that I have the utmost respect.

Fortunately, I have developed techniques that keep that respect in check and that enhance the magic in the personal and spiritual connection that transpires.

Characterists of a Caring Clown

As a result of my NLP training and techniques I learned at Clown Camp, I developed certain behaviors that help me connect with others.

1) You must "listen" with all of your senses: hear what the person is saying, i.e. – *content* as well as *how* they speak. Is the other person's voice high or low? Soft or loud? Raspy or clear? Quick or slow? Next, see what the other person is doing, i.e. – look at the person's facial expression; notice gestures and posture; pay attention to how you feel when you are with the person. This may give you a clue for how the other person is feeling.

2) When you first meet someone, pay attention to the information you get from all of your senses. What do you see, hear, taste, smell, and touch?

3) Since I am a psychotherapist, I am very aware of how many people do not want to be touched. It's kind of sad actually. Anyway, I always ask people if they want a hug before I give one. I will offer my hand, and if they choose, they will take it. If not, I respect their wish.

4) Before I interact with someone I make sure that I have a referral, which can come from the patient/resident, from staff, or from a visitor/family member. Then the person still has the last word as to whether he or she is up for this kind of company. I particularly look for eye contact when I walk in the halls. If someone does not look at me, then I respect the other person's space and keep on going. I do not want to force the interaction.

5) I use all of the information I gather through my senses and try to mirror back as best I can what I sense in order to establish a connection. By practicing these rapport skills, I'm able to "see" with my ears, "hear" through my eyes, and "touch" with my heart.

Ho-Ho-Ha-Ha-Ha

One integral part of HA!HA!LOGY is the Laughter Club. These occur weekly in various units at the Hebrew Home. Residents who choose to participate meet at regular appointed times to take part in the laughter exercise workout and other activities that encourage playfulness, fun, and mental balance. It's a social, physical, and emotional experience for them.

My Laughter Club is modeled after Dr. Kataria's. While we do some of the exercises exactly as Dr. Kataria devised them, I have taken liberty to modify some of them according to my own views and teachings and the residents' capabilities.

We begin each Laughter Club session with breathing exercises. All the residents are seated, and I instruct them to take a deep breath in and to raise their hands as far above their heads as they possibly can. Those who have difficulty raising their hands are instructed not to, as Steve Wilson's motto (which I've adopted too) throughout the entire exercise is "no pain…no pain." For those who can't raise their hands, I encourage them to make a picture in their mind of what they would look like if they were fully participating in the exercise. While that may sound silly, it's just as effective as actually doing the exercise, because our brains and bodies don't know the difference between thinking about doing something and actually doing it. The power of visualization is a remarkable internal motivator.

I then ask the participants to loudly say "Aaah" as they release their breath (which encourages a good healthy laugh) and allow their hands to come down to their laps.† We do that for several inhalations and exhalations.* And that's just the beginning!

Like a finely-tuned choir, we all clap our hands and chant in unison, "Ho-Ho-Ha-Ha-Ha! Ho-Ho-Ha-Ha-Ha!"* We do several stanzas of these, as it's our Laughter Club mantra. It's also how we warm up for our laughter exercises.* The clapping has significance, too. Across the palms of our hands, we each have acupressure points. When we clap and touch our palms together, we stimulate those points and help balance the body's energy.

Once we complete the initial breathing and chanting, we begin the actual laughing exercises. The first one, which is a great warm up, is called the Cocktail Party Laugh.** For those who don't drink, I guess you could also call it the High Tea Laugh.† Have you ever noticed that when you go to cocktail parties or afternoon teas some people may not act naturally and their laughs sound forced? Well, that's what this exercise

† - Exercise developed by Jacki Kwan
* - Exercise developed by Dr. Kataria
** - Exercise developed by Steve Wilson

exaggerates. I go around from participant to participant and laugh with them in this phony way. You know, it's that nasal sounding, "e-Heh, e-Heh, e-Heh," kind of laugh. After making my rounds, I encourage the participants to look into each other's eyes and laugh, which magnifies the fun.

At the end of the exercise, we do more deep breathing and chanting of the "Ho-Ho-Ha-Ha-Ha! Ho-Ho-Ha-Ha-Ha!" mantra.

From there we move into the Humming Laugh.* This one is fairly simple. While most people laugh with a "Ha-Ha-Ha," the humming laugh encourages people to laugh with a "Hmmm-Hmmm-Hmmm." Again I make my rounds and give each person the individualized attention he or she deserves. Some of the residents choose not to look at each other. Most will, however, interact with me. Once complete, we do more breathing and chanting.

My favorite laughing exercise comes next. It's the Ice Cube Down the Back Laugh.** Have you ever been the recipient of the "ice cube down the back" prank? If so, then you know the laugh I'm talking about. It goes something like, "Eee-hee-hee-hee! Eee-hee-hee-hee!"

There are many other kinds of laughs we do, such as the Bare Feet on Hot Concrete Laugh,** the Roller Coaster Laugh,** the Lion Laugh,* and the Argumentative Laugh.* By far the most popular and most enjoyable laughing exercise the participants do is the Conductor Laugh.† I begin by explaining that the reason why orchestra conductors live so long is that they spend the majority of their time with their hands above their heart. As they're conducting their orchestra and flailing their arms, they're stimulating blood flow to all parts of their body. While I don't expect any of my participants to move their arms like a music conductor, I do want them to take advantage of some of the health benefits of the conductor's lifestyle with the Conductor Laugh.

We begin with our hands in the air as if we were about to conduct a live symphony orchestra. I frequently take a pen or a chopstick if I have one and tap on one of the resident's walkers to ready our "orchestra!" Then, to the tune of "Blue Danube," we slowly and rhythmically move our arms as we sing, "Dah-dah-dah-dah-dah – Ha-Ha! Ha-Ha! Dah-dah-dah-dah-dah – Ha-Ha! Ha-Ha!" And the entire melody carries on from there. By the time we're done, everyone is relaxed and singing and in a positive state of mind. I love to sing, but I can't carry a tune. So many laugh as I belt out the melody off key!

One of my most favorite moments of Laughter Club is when the participants begin to laugh uncontrollably for no apparent reason. That's when they get the full benefit of Laughter Therapy. At first they feel silly for laughing so hard, and then I explain why laughing like that is a good thing. "It's good for your heart, your lungs, and your immune system," I tell them. Some of them believe me, and some don't. That's okay. As long as they're laughing, they're momentarily forgetting about any pain – both physical and emotional – in their lives, so whether or not they believe my reasons for encouraging laughter is irrelevant.

I conclude each Laughter Club session with cheers* – positive affirmations designed to keep people in good humor. I instruct them to repeat these cheers even if they don't believe them to be true. "If it isn't true, then pretend," I say. I find that if they pretend for even a nanosecond, then the cheer will become true.

For the first cheer, I tell them to throw their arms in the air as high as they can and shout, "I am the happiest person in the world! Yes!"

The second cheer makes them proclaim, "I am the healthiest person in the world! Yes!"

And the last cheer says, "I am a Hebrew Home Laugher! Yes!"

The final part of the Laughter Club session is when I hand out funny stickers and hugs.† However, I never force either of these items on people. I have a strict "I Pass" rule that states if a participant doesn't want a sticker or hug, he or she just has to say so and I respect that decision.

I do think the stickers are important, though, because they give the participants a physical reminder of their experience in Laughter Club. During future moments when they may feel depressed or as if no one cares about them, all they have to do is look at their sticker and they can recall the fun time they had at Laughter Club. It's a catalyst for bringing them back into the positive state of mind they create during a Humor Therapy session.

A Laughter Club Success Story

When I first started leading Laughter Club sessions at the Hebrew Home, I met one man who was a Holocaust survivor. I don't know the specifics of his past experiences, but I imagine they must have been awful, as he was bitter, sour, and disruptive during Laughter Club sessions. "How can you people laugh when things like World War II happened?" he would interrupt. "How can you be happy knowing that people were tortured needlessly?" He thought it was absolutely ridiculous that anyone could be happy, even if for only a brief moment. To him, laughing was almost sacrilege.

Because of his disruptive behavior, I was at the point where I needed to ask staff members to help me control him. We calmly explained to him that he either had to leave the group or he had to sit there quietly and behave. There were other people present who greatly wanted to participate, and his outbursts were ruining the experience for the group. He agreed to leave, and for the next year and a half I avoided him as much as possible. When I saw him in the halls, I didn't make eye contact, as it was his nature to glare at me. I didn't want to encourage his behavior, plus I didn't want his negative energy to be a drain on my emotional resources.

One morning in the summer of 2001, I was walking the halls of the Hebrew Home, and there he was, almost as if he were waiting for me. I was dressed as Elfinya, and I knew my clown outfit would irritate him. I tried to turn away so I wouldn't run into him, but he followed me, the whole time shouting his litany of anti-laughter and World War II horror stories. I knew I had to say something to calm him, so I replied, "I think I have an idea where you're coming from, and I respect that. And I also know that humor isn't always appropriate. It's a matter of balance, and just because you laugh sometimes doesn't take the other stuff away." He stopped, thought about what I said, nodded, and then walked away.

Later that day as I began setting up for Laughter Club, he came into the room and sat down. I saw him and I froze. The little voice inside me said, "Oh no! Now what do I do?" Then it was as if I had a little Saint sitting on one shoulder and a little Devil on the other. The Devil spoke first and said, "I can't believe he's here. Call the staff. We're going to have to set limits on his behavior. He upsets all the residents. They think he's crazy. He's going to be disruptive. Do something to get him out of here. Quick!"

Then the Saint chimed in: "He's probably very lonely. He has probably alienated everyone in this place because of his attitude. Just give him a chance."

The internal struggle went back and forth for what seemed like an eternity. A few moments later I regained control of my thoughts and decided to treat him just like I treat all the other participants. As people started to trickle in, I made it a point to personally greet each one. I couldn't leave him out of the greeting, so I went up to him and said, "Welcome."

He sat there and didn't respond. As I stood before him, I felt myself shrink back into my former childlike self. I suddenly felt so inadequate. I wanted nothing more than to run from the room and never return. Luckily, the grown-up part of me took control and shouted, "Stop it! You're an adult and these people need you. So work your magic."

I agreed with the adult part of me. After I greeted everyone, we began the breathing and chanting exercises. As I

led the group through "Ho-Ho-Ha-Ha-Ha! Ho-Ho-Ha-Ha-Ha!"
I looked over to the man. To my astonishment, he was clapping
and chanting with the rest of us. I was so excited. That little
voice inside me shouted, "Hot damn!"

I continued the session as usual, interacting with him
just as I did with the other participants. When the session was
over, I went around and asked each person whether he or she
wanted a sticker and/or a hug. As I approached him, I looked
straight into his eyes and asked as sweetly as I could, "Would
you like a sticker?"

Slowly he said, "Yes."

I was so blown away! The entire time I knew him all I
ever heard come from his mouth were erudite statements using
words I didn't even understand. And here he was accepting a
silly little sticker! Then he pulled me close and said to me,
"You're a special person." At that instant, it was as if time
stood still. I couldn't believe my ears and had to take a moment
to catch my breath.

I then asked him, "Would you like a hug?"

"No thank you," he replied.

I was okay with that. He wasn't ready for a hug, and I
respected that. After the group cleared he stayed and struck up
a conversation with me. As soon as he opened his mouth, I
wanted to bolt the other way, as I was expecting his former self
to resurface, but I reassured myself that this would be a great
opportunity to connect with him.

I thanked him for coming to Laughter Club and for
participating. Then we sat in silence. I didn't know what to say
next. I knew I couldn't talk to him about history or his past
because it would bring up negative emotions. For some reason
he brought up the topic of Freud. I thought, "Ha-Ha! I may not
know about history, but I know about Freud."

I began to explain how Freud wrote some treatises on
the value of humor as a very sophisticated defense mechanism.
As I spoke, he listened intently, and I felt the whole energy of

our interaction shift from uneasiness to comfort. For that brief conversation, our spirits connected and we formed a bond that no negative energy could penetrate.

Working with him that day was a major turning point in my career. I knew that I could work with challenging people and have a positive effect on their life. Thanks to him, I no longer regard these types of "people challenges" as negative events; they're my soul food and an important part of my spiritual journey home.

Chapter Four

Laugh! There Are No Toxic Side Effects

"The art of medicine consists of keeping the patient amused while nature heals the disease." – Voltaire

For thousands of years, scientists, philosophers, and psychologists have touted the health-enhancing benefits of laughter. As far back as biblical times, scholars have stated that a merry heart works like a doctor. In more recent analysis, the scientific world has examined humor and found that mirthful laughter – that is, the laughter associated with positive humor – has an effect on most of the major physiologic body systems. Lab experiments have demonstrated that laughter positively affects the respiratory system, the cardiovascular system, the muscular system, the central nervous system, the endocrine system, and the immune system. To the best of my knowledge, none of the experiments have noted any negative side effects that are so often associated with traditional medical treatments.

When we speak of the health benefits of laughter, it's important to clearly establish a definition of "Therapeutic Humor." According to the Association for Applied and Therapeutic Humor (AATH), Therapeutic Humor is defined to be "any intervention that promotes health and wellness by stimulating a playful discovery, expression, or appreciation of the absurdity or incongruity of life's situations. This intervention may enhance health or be used as a complementary treatment of illness to facilitate healing or coping, whether physical, emotional, cognitive, social, or spiritual." Armed with that definition, we can now begin to explore the many wonderful health benefits laughter can help people experience.

Wisdom of the Ages

Four hundred years ago, Robert Burton wrote an essay entitled *Anatomy of Melancholy*. In it, he observed that "humor purges the blood, making the body young, lively, and fit for any manner of employment." He concluded that laughter is the best defense for "battering the walls of melancholy…and a sufficient cure in itself."

In his *Critique of Pure Reason*, 18th century philosopher Immanuel Kant wrote that laughter produces a "feeling of health through the furtherance of the vital bodily processes, the affection that moves the intestines and the diaphragms; in a word, the feeling of health that makes up the gratification felt by us; so that we can thus reach the body through the soul and use the latter as the physician of the former."

Sigmund Freud, too, believed in the healing power of laughter. He wrote that laughter was a highly useful way of counteracting nervous tension, and that humor could be used as effective therapy. He once stated, "Like wit and the comic, humor has a liberating element. It is the triumph of narcissism, the ego's victorious assertion of its own invulnerability. It refuses to suffer the slings and arrows of reality."

More recently, Norman Cousins, former editor for *Saturday Review*, brought up the possibility that laughter may have healing potential. In 1964, Cousins was diagnosed with Ankylosing Spondylitis, a progressive degenerative and potentially fatal connective tissue disease. His physicians suggested that exposure to heavy metal poisoning was the cause of his condition. Traditional medicine gave him little hope for recovery, so Cousins decided to take matters into his own hands.

Cousins recalled reading that negative emotions could trigger chemical body changes that could lead to adrenal exhaustion – what he suspected weakened his body's ability to tolerate toxic exposure. He also suspected that positive emotions, like joy, faith, and hope, could reverse the negative effects of his disease. Since laughing tends to open people up to positive emotions, Cousins began viewing funny films to stimulate laughter. He found that 10 minutes of mirthful laughter allowed him to experience two full hours of pain-free sleep. He also discovered that laughter stimulated a decrease in his sedimentation rate, indicating a reversal of the inflammatory response his disease triggered. After his recovery, Cousins spent the last ten years of his life as an adjunct professor at U.C.L.A. Medical School, where he established a Humor Task Force to coordinate and support clinical research.

Modern Day Humor Wisdom

Since Cousins' breakthrough, other researchers have studied humor. Dr. William Fry, a psychiatrist from Stanford University, found that a person could get much good physical exercise through laughter. He also cited that laughter stimulates the cardiovascular system, increases heart rate and circulation, and lowers blood pressure. Also, because laughter speeds the body's respiration rate, residual air built up in the lungs, along with water vapor, are expelled during laughter, thereby lessening the chance of respiratory infection.

Some of the most exciting research regarding laughter's potential healing value is in the field of psychoneuroimmunology, which explores the connections between the nervous system (where thought, memory, and emotions generate), the endocrine system (our hormone center), and the immune system (the body's natural defense mechanism against illness). While at Loma Linda University Medical Center, Dr. Lee Berk completed research showing that laughter affects the neuroendocrine system. His work has documented that serum cortisol and epinephrine levels (both known to be immunosuppressive) increase with stress, yet decrease with laughter. Therefore, Dr. Berk concluded that by decreasing these levels people could diminish the suppression of the immune components. To put it in simpler terms, laughter increases the concentration of circulating antibodies in the blood stream. It also increases the concentration of circulating white blood cells in the immune reaction to combat foreign proteins. These changes make you more resistant to developing infection. It doesn't mean you won't get an infection, yet it does increase your resistance level.

Also in 1997, Dr. Berk studied 24 post heart attack patients. All were treated with standard medical care and cardiac rehabilitation. Dr. Berk invited half the patients to watch a humorous video of their choice for 30 minutes each day. The other half did not receive the Humor Therapy. After one year, the humor treated patients had less arrhythmias, lower blood pressure, and lower levels of stress hormones. They required lower doses of beta-blocker medication, and they had a decreased need for nitroglycerin. Only 20% of the Humor Therapy group had a recurrent heart attack, compared to 50% in the usual care group. Clearly, Therapeutic Humor has merit.

Humor Can Soothe the Weary Body

Scientists have known for many years that the human brain excretes a substance called endorphins – a substance very much like morphine in its molecular structure and effects. When the human body is exposed to sudden pain, such as if we are in a car accident, the brain releases these endorphins as a natural painkiller and relaxant. It's our body's natural defense mechanism during shock. Dr. Fry and Dr. Dale Anderson found that the human body produces endorphin-like reactions during mirthful laughter, thus causing our perception of pain to diminish.

In another study, Kathleen Dillon at Western New England College found an increase of IgA (immunoglobulin A – our first line of defense against the entry of infectious organisms through the respiratory tract) present during laughter. Dr. Berk duplicated this finding, as he found that showing patients humorous videos increased their concentration of salivary IgA. This research proves that the mind (emotions) and the body (immune system) are interrelated.

One of the most fascinating studies Dr. Berk conducted involved Positron Emission Test (PET) scans, which measure people's brainwaves. He found that people in mirthful laughter exhibit the same brainwaves of those in a meditative state. So laughter is not only good for physical health, but it's also good for emotional health as it helps us relax and release tension.

Finally, when asked his views on the importance of humor to well being, renowned author, researcher, and doctor Deepak Chopra responded, "Human beings are the only species that crack jokes. They're also the only species aware of their mortality, and therefore the paradox of experience. Humor allows us to go beyond the pulls of opposite and get in touch with the core of our being. The pulls of opposite, such as sacred and profane, sinner and saint, divine and diabolical create conflict in the mind. Humor allows us to go beyond all of that and get in touch with our soul. It is now known through good research that humor changes our physiology and biochemistry and evokes the healing response. In fact, the chemicals in the tears of laughter are quite different from the tears of sadness and suffering. More research needs to be done in this area, but my personal belief is that God must be a humorist and that the universe is her idea of a cosmic joke."

Well said!!

So now there's absolutely no reason not to laugh, laugh, laugh! There are no known toxic side effects, and it's absolutely free. You can even fake a smile if you don't feel like laughing and still get health benefits. You can choose to fake it till you make it... or not.

Humor and Our Emotional Well Being

Humor and laughter affect how we perceive events around us and how we react to change. The fact is that we each have a choice for how we deal with stressful life events, whether they be due to illness, work, or relationships. The event itself is neutral – it is neither good nor bad. Our reaction to the event is what determines whether we perceive it as a positive or negative experience.

For example, suppose you're stopped at a traffic light when you feel a hard knock against the back of your car. You look up in your rearview mirror and see that someone has rear-ended you. It's just a minor fender bender, so you and the person behind you pull over to the side. The fact that a minor car accident occurred is in itself a neutral event. Whether you choose to rant and rave about it or politely exchange car insurance information is up to you. You and you alone have the ultimate choice as to whether or not this event will ruin your day and put you in a negative state of mind. Those people who can get out of the car and force a good hearty laugh will have a hard time yelling at the other driver, thus forcing themselves to view the event with a positive outlook.

Herbert Lefcourt, a noted psychologist from the University of Waterloo in Canada, has conducted research to determine whether or not a sense of humor can alter our emotional response to stress. In his study, he evaluated patients' frequency and severity of stressful life changes that occurred over the previous six months. He then evaluated the patients' negative mood disturbances in relation to those events. Lefcourt administered psychological tests to evaluate the patients' use of humor, perception of humor, appreciation of laughter, and efforts to include humor and laughter into their day. His results showed that the patients who could sense and appreciate humor were able to buffer the negative mood disturbances they felt in response to the stressful life event.

Because laughter is a pleasurable experience, it helps us to momentarily release feelings of anger and fear. When we laugh, we feel lighthearted, carefree, and hopeful. These emotions help us gain a new perspective on the challenge we're facing and enable us to feel in control of the situation.

I recently came across a remarkable news article that reported on a new device designed to help people who suffer from depression. The device, which is the size of a pocket watch and similar to a pacemaker, is implanted in the patient's chest. Wires attach the device to the vagus nerve, which runs from the neck into a mysterious part of the brain thought to control mood and emotion. The vagus nerve relays messages back and forth between the brain and other organs and regulates automatic bodily functions. Every few minutes the device stimulates the vagus nerve, causing it to act more normally. Apparently the device is helping people combat depression by triggering laughter. When asked if he was being forced to laugh or if he just felt good inside, one patient responded, "Both."

This new treatment has worked on half of the 30 patients involved in the pilot study. The results of this study are not definitive and still require more research, but I believe they look promising for the future of Humor Therapy.

A Childlike Approach to Good Humor

Have you ever noticed that children are constantly laughing? They laugh on average 60 times a day. Do you know how many times per day the average adult laughs? Only 10. Somewhere through the years we seem to forget that laughing makes us feel good and washes away the pressures of the day-to-day routine.

While I was working at the hospital I met a little girl in the pediatric unit who exemplified to me how our perception of an event shapes our attitude. The little girl was probably only eight years old. As a result of a dog bite, she had severe lacerations on her face, the worst being near her mouth. She had a significant amount of swelling, which made it impossible for her to smile with both sides of her mouth. When she did smile, it reminded me of someone who recently had a Novocain injection, as her smile was lopsided.

The girl, her mother, and I were in the playroom chatting about their stay in the hospital. The girl's mother then said to her daughter, "I bet you can't wait to get home." The little girl quickly responded that she absolutely did NOT want to leave the hospital. When I asked her why, she said in total seriousness, "Because I have my own phone here."

What a wonderful attitude! This little eight-year-old girl had the incredible ability to see something positive about her experience and she chose to focus on that positive aspect in order to make her experience a happy one. Her story reminds me of something Joel Goodman, Director of the Humor Project, told me. "Choosing to improve your sense of humor prevents hardening of the attitudes." How's that for a profound statement! In my day-to-day interactions with people, I carry Joel Goodman's message on by encouraging people to reconnect with their curious, creative, and whimsical internal child in order to promote their own healthy psychological mindset.

Increase Your Dosage

Researchers around the world agree: much more needs to be done in regards to humor research. It's funny to me that "research" is needed. We *know* when we feel better. Some need the research, though, to demonstrate the true effects a positive state of mind has on the body. Its seems a little co-dependent to wait until someone tells us how to feel before we feel that way!

Unfortunately, many doctors have a difficult time using humor when they treat patients. They believe their role is to be "serious" and the "voice of reason" during a medical crisis. While it's true that patients don't want to think their doctors arc fooling around and missing key medical clues that could alleviate their condition, patients do want doctors who are friendly and lighthearted, who know how to strike a balance between seriousness and humor. They want to feel at ease and as comfortable as possible when facing a medical situation.

For those of you who want to benefit from Therapeutic Humor every day, the prescription is simple: Laugh! Don't wait until you hear or see something funny. Begin to see the world from a new perspective by putting on your funny glasses and finding the humor in everyday situations. And when something negative does happen, remember an old saying one of my clients repeatedly says, "Ca-ca occurs!" Then, laugh about it. Release the uncomfortable emotions you want to dispel, and open yourself up to a positive and hopeful mindset. With a little practice, you'll soon find that your humorous outlook is contagious, and you can cause a laughter epidemic.

Rock and Roll!

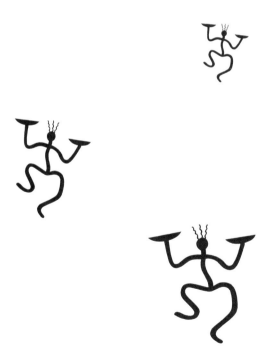

Chapter Five

Heroes of the Home

"Laughter is the shortest distance between two people."
–Victor Borge

Each day that I work as a Therapeutic Clown I become more and more amazed with the people I meet and the resilience of their spirit. Many of the people I interact with are suffering from debilitating illnesses or are dying, yet they have the courage to be strong and are able to inspire others despite their own challenges. I call such people my "heroes," as they have unknowingly inspired me to do what I do.

Because of my chaotic childhood and the fact that I received little attention from my parents when I was young, I grew up not feeling very worthwhile or important. I always doubted myself, and I used my sense of humor as way to mask that inner pain. As I got older, those feelings intensified, leaving me with low self-esteem. By the time I reached adulthood, I was constantly struggling with feelings of depression. Although I may have been laughing on the outside, on the inside I was crying for relief.

I remember waking up many mornings with a feeling of dread overpowering my mind and body. Regardless of what I had planned to do on those days, I couldn't muster the strength to get out of bed. I'd lie there with the covers pulled over my head and wish there were a way I could overcome the awful feelings, but I couldn't. The emotional pain was just too great for me to bear. I'd give in to my feelings and remain alone in my room, depressed and tired, for the entire day. Ultimately I'd waste one of the most precious gifts – the gift of today – because I couldn't find the strength to feel my way out of my mental darkness.

By watching and learning from the patients at the hospital and the residents at the Hebrew Home (and many years of therapy!), I can now see, hear, and feel what true strength and courage are. The will to live these people display on a daily basis makes me realize that each day is precious and a special gift I must savor. Working with the residents is like medicine for me. Whenever I wake up and feel out of balance or as if I'm struggling with my depression, I think of the challenges the residents are facing, and suddenly my own spirit lifts as I have the overwhelming desire to interact with them and take them from their pain. Their heroic actions to face the day no matter what teach me the true joy of life and help me see the path I know I must follow.

Although I encounter many such heroes every day, three in particular stand out in my mind. I'd like to share with you my experiences with them. I hope they inspire you as much as they've inspired me.

My First Experience With an Angel

In March of 1999 I met my first of many heroes. I was working in the oncology unit at the hospital. That particular day I was visiting people as my "painter" character. I wore my hospital volunteer jacket along with a painter's cap. For my props I carried a paint bucket with a paintbrush and a supply of "Dry Paint" signs.

As was protocol at the hospital, I first went to the nurse's station and asked who they thought might like a visit from me. The nurses on duty unanimously suggested that I visit a man, whom I'll call "Paul," in room 304. They told me he had advanced cancer and was feeling very sick due to his radiation and chemotherapy treatments.

I walked down the hall to room 304, knocked on the door, and then walked in offering my usual cheery, "Morning!"

I saw Paul seated in the chair by his bedside. He looked tired, and the gray bathrobe he wore seemed to match the color of his face. Despite his obvious lack of physical strength, Paul took one look at me and started laughing hysterically. As he laughed, the color rushed back to his cheeks. Seeing this sick man enjoy the moment lit the spark for a lifetime connection.

Once Paul stopped laughing, I asked him if he wanted a "Dry Paint" sign. He said yes, so I took my paintbrush out of my paint can and pretended to paint him. With each stroke of the brush, Paul laughed some more. When I was done, I stuck a "Dry Paint" sign on him. Paul thought this little exercise was the most hysterical thing in the world. He thanked me for brightening his day and asked when I could see him again.

Since I was volunteering at the hospital three days a week, I visited Paul each day I was there. And every time I'd see him I'd leave him with some kind of sticker or physical memento of my visit. He'd proudly display each item on his closet door, and before long the various items overtook his once barren room.

During my visits he and I would talk about various topics ranging from family to religion to careers. One day while I was struggling with a decision about how I should structure my Humor Therapy program, Paul gave me some life-changing advice. At this point I was not yet a clown and the whole concept of HA!HA!LOGY was not fully formulated. As I spoke with Paul, I expressed my concerns of designing a Therapeutic Humor program and how I thought I first must be an official clown to proceed. Paul looked at me, took my hand, and said, "You're doing great. You're doing exactly what you should be doing in life. You don't have to be a clown. Just do what you're doing, follow your personality, and structure the program around who you are. You can do it! Go for it!"

His words were so simple, yet they were precisely what I needed to hear at the time. Here was this sick and dying man encouraging me to live my life in a way no one had ever done before. Instead of being bitter and sad about his situation, he chose to invite laughter into his life and to offer hope to others. What a hero!

Paul has since died, but to this day his words still ring in my ears. And whenever I have a choice to make about my HA1HA!LOGY! program, I think of what Paul said to me and I find the strength and courage to trust my own judgment. I am so grateful that Paul was a part of my life and I feel extremely blessed that our spirits were able to connect.

A Courageous Spirit

If I ever begin to question the resiliency of the human spirit, all I have to do is think of Mary Ann. At age 55, Mary Ann is one of the youngest residents at the Hebrew Home. Because of her long-term battle against Rheumatoid Arthritis, she is wheelchair bound and requires the level of constant care the Hebrew Home offers.

Incidentally, I first met Mary Ann at the hospital. She was sitting inside the hospital visitor's lounge one day after receiving treatment for some bilateral ankle ulcers when I walked by in my vividly colored clown costume. I think Mary Ann describes the situation best when she says, "Through the thick glass windows I saw a bundle of bright purple, canary yellow, and orange with a giggle and a grin coming towards the automatic front door. I thought to myself, 'Wow! This woman is a weirdo. She's my kind of person!'" Thus began our deep and spiritual connection with each other.

Mary Ann and I interacted as often as possible. I learned she was being admitted to the Hebrew Home around the same time I began working there. Was fate doing its job of keeping us together? I certainly think so.

Mary Ann has a special energy that comes from somewhere deep within herself. One day I asked her about her past and what kind of challenges she's had to overcome. As she explained her story to me, her twinkling large eyes and broad smile diminished. When she was young, her father was murdered – bludgeoned to death – leaving her mother the sole guidance for her and her brother. As never before, the devastated and scarred family was challenged to carry on with far less than ever anticipated.

In the 1960s, after her brother worked in the engineering field for three years, he went to fight in Vietnam. He returned with post-traumatic stress disorder. Mary Ann did her best to help her brother emotionally, and in the years that followed she watched him suffer through a heart attack and then triple bypass surgery. Soon after that experience, Mary Ann's mother died, and then Mary Ann learned she had Rheumatoid Arthritis complicated by vascular disease. However, throughout all the trials, Mary Ann was determined to make something of herself and not fall victim to circumstances.

She worked her way through college to obtain a degree in Psychology. As part of her studies, she interviewed samples of male students within the community as well as in rehabilitation schools to investigate the nature of aggression. From compiled test data, she designed and wrote an experiment that ultimately shaped her thesis. Again, however, illness, coupled with extensive physical therapy, pre-empted continuing studies that would have led to a doctorate in clinical psychology.

As I sat in awe listening to her story, I had to ask her, "How did you survive? How did you keep your will to live?"

She responded, "As I reflected on my life, I realized there is an internal faith ever present. It not only motivates me, but it also propels me forward. As a result, I am filled with strength and peace. This peace involves a communion with God. So I began to understand that whatever I want to do in life, I must have a prayer in my heart and a great passion for any mission. I now feel deeply that my mission is to help others in any manner I can.

"In retrospect, I realize all these events happened for a reason. They were preparation for the future. I'm certain that God wanted me to grow and mature at a pace different from one I would have chosen. I know how to be patient with life now. I have reconciled all those hurtful experiences.

"In the first half of my life, I was very patient with other people, but not with myself. I always felt that I should have accomplished things sooner than I actually did. I felt I should have finished college sooner, should have started on my doctorate sooner, should have gotten a job sooner, should have married sooner, etc. I thought all those events would come in some sort of natural sequence. Rather, life experiences are ongoing, and sometimes it's hit and miss. To be all you can be, find your passion. It will energize and fulfill you. Also, you must throw problems over your back and stand tall and step on them.

"Actually I don't accept the word 'problem.' It's not in my active vocabulary. Rather, I try to summon all my strength to face challenges. Incidentally, humor has always been a part of me. I feel humor is a synergy between our energy and strength. So I have used humor to some degree in all my difficult times, for it allowed me to move over harsh and jagged edges while preserving my dignity and not sacrificing to complacency."

Hearing someone else express her belief in the power of humor was an enlightening experience for me. Mary Ann is a well-educated woman who has studied and worked in the psychology field. She revealed how she has always been fascinated with the mind/body connection – how our behaviors affect our state of mind and vice-versa.

During her studies, she learned that when people are unhappy, it negatively influences their autonomic system, their metabolism, their nerve endings, and their nerve synapses. People become tense; their muscles constrict. On the other hand, she explained that when people laugh or feel some joy, there's a sense of release. This feeling of joy makes them feel lighter in every aspect. There is a tension reduction. Laughing gives people a more hopeful outlook, and while they may not completely overcome the challenge they're facing, they will be better able to cope with the stress they are feeling.

Her sentiments were all things I had already believed, and hearing another person express them without prompting from me was like a calling to my soul that I was on the right path. I immediately invited Mary Ann to participate in my next Laughter Club session at the Hebrew Home, and she agreed. Having her in the room with me that day during Laughter Club enlivened the entire group. It was like having an assistant to spread joy to the residents who were hurting.

The most inspiring aspect of Mary Ann is when I speak to her about her medical condition. After eight consecutive years of hospitalization and numerous surgeries, her ulcers have healed. I guess that's why she always makes it a point of stating, "I have Rheumatoid Arthritis; the Rheumatoid Arthritis doesn't have me."

When I ask her what she means by that she says, "My movement may be hard to see right now, but I am definitely moving forward. I'm not going to be in this particular position much longer. I've been in a wheelchair before. I've had such a bad overall arthritic breakdown that I couldn't even hold an empty teacup. I've had fevers in all my joints. Because of all the medications, I've developed bilateral ulcers and gangrene from having broken veins, which decreased my blood/oxygen flow to the affected areas. But you know what? That's all behind me. I'm moving forward. I've decided to throw all my problems over both shoulders and onto the ground so I can roll over top of them. That's what you have to do if you want to move forward.

"I believe that you cannot climb a smooth mountain. You must have crevices in that mountain in order to propel yourself forward. And as you are going forward, it's important to remember where you came from and the fact that you are not in that circumstance anymore. You can move forward because all those things are behind you now. This is not to say that those past events weren't painful and hurtful. It's just that those past events are less important than what is in front of you now.

"I hope that the fact that I am moving forward in good spirit and faith can help someone else who perhaps has lost all faith. I believe this internal faith passes all understanding and will carry you through any situation. I hope my actions can inspire others to move forward. So often it's what we do rather than what we say that encourages people to action. You never know who's watching you. That's why I always keep a positive attitude and stay focused on my goal. The smaller I make my line of focus, the more my energy generates. It becomes like a laser beam, and laser beams can cut through steel. With an attitude like that, how can I not persevere?"

Mary Ann's amazing attitude inspires me every day. And her never-ending internal fountain of joy is an inspiration to all Hebrew Home residents. Mary Ann is my humor ambassador on the days I'm not at the Home, and her example is a constant source of strength for me every day of my life. I believe our spirits will forever be connected, and I treasure every moment I have with Mary Ann. She is a hero in every sense of the word and a living testament to the power of Therapeutic Humor.

Unending Resolve

While so many residents touch my spirit every day, none do it so profoundly as Tina Jasen, a lady who has been battling the devastating effects of multiple sclerosis for over 33 years. Despite the fact that she can only move her face, head, and three fingers on her right hand, Tina has an amazing attitude that exudes positivity. She claims that the reason she wants to be so strong is so she can set an example for her kids and grandkids that no matter how bad it gets you can still thrive with a positive attitude. Wow!

I look forward to seeing Tina each week. She's the first resident I visit every time I go to her building. Her courage is so strong that it's like a brilliant white light radiating from her room. I feel it even before I set foot in there.

I have this ritual that I do before I enter her room. I stand at her doorway, knock, say "knock-knock," and then I blow bubbles into her room. She knows it's me when she sees the bubbles. As I slowly enter her room, the first thing I see are her feet peeking around the corner. I take a few more steps, and there she is. She immediately greets me with her "loud" smile. My smile echoes hers. As soon as we're together in her room, I feel our spiritual connection. It's like a warmth that radiates from everything in the room.

When I visit, she's usually sitting in her wheelchair and wearing a regal colored robe of purple and fuchsia. She always has bright red lipstick on. In fact, I've never seen her without lipstick! I always think it's amazing that given all of her challenges, she still wants her hair combed neatly and has the grace to wear lipstick too.

The first thing she always says to me is, "Hello, darling." The way she says "darling" sounds more like "dahling," with a broad "a," and reminds me of how my mom used to talk. I melt each time I hear it. Because of her MS, she speaks softly, almost in a whisper. I often find myself whispering too. It's how I've built rapport with her over the years. As we talk, she often giggles. I realized one day that she giggles just like my mom used to. In other conversations we've had she's told me that she used to work on Capitol Hill as a personal assistant for one of the Members of Congress. My mom worked on the Hill as well. In fact, Tina knew my mom's boss. Every time I'm with Tina I realize just how much I miss my mother. Being with her is like truly coming home.

When I ask Tina about her incredibly positive attitude, she simply says, "Life has given me strength and has taught me humility. God may have taken a part of my life away, but he has given me a lot more – my precious children, my darling (dahling) husband, and my 16 grandchildren. I used to be angry because of my illness, but now I'm accepting of it."

Each time I visit her we talk about her family. I look at all the family photos that adorn her walls and ask her about various people. She always tells me that her children are her heroes, as is her husband. "My husband and I were married 36 years," she says. "He died six years ago. That's when I came here to the Home. My children live too far away to take care of me. I miss my husband very much, but I talk to him every day. He was a funny man. He used to write jokes. I absolutely loved his jokes. They always made me laugh. And with an illness like mine, you need a sense of humor to tolerate the disability.

"I believe that laughter is an antidote for anything. If you can laugh at yourself and things around you, then you can maintain a healthy attitude. I feel sorry for people who can't find the humor in themselves and the things around them. I don't think God put us here to cry. I think God put us here to enjoy every single minute that we can. When I laugh, I momentarily forget about my pain and discomfort."

I could sit and listen to Tina all day. She always has words of wisdom that invigorate my spirit and inspire me to keep going. One day while I was visiting with her she asked me to write cards for two of her grandchildren who had their Bar and Bat Mitzvah the previous month. I agreed and wrote down the words she dictated.

I then handed her the pen so she could sign the cards. Remember, the MS has destroyed her nerves to the point that she only has use of her face, head, and three fingers on her right hand. As she took the pen, it pained me to see her struggle to make it work. As she began to sign the first card, she stopped and said that she had forgotten how to write. I told her to take her time and breathe…that it would come back to her. At that point I down shifted into my slowest gear. I felt so much sadness that she was struggling, and although I desperately wanted to offer her help, I didn't. I wanted my energy to say that I knew she could do it.

Lo and behold…she did it! I was ecstatic, and so was she. The second card was easier for her. I didn't say anything about my sense of relief that she did it. We're so connected, though, that I think she could tell anyway. Seeing Tina's unending resolve is soul food for me. It's people like her who give me the confidence to truly be me.

Unsuspecting Heroes

Such positive people like Paul, Mary Ann, and Tina affect my life in so many ways. However, there are many other residents who impact my life with both their positive and negative actions. I call such people my "unsuspecting heroes," because it is often only after I look back and reexamine the events that I realize how important those people are to my spiritual awakening.

One example of this is a lady I'll call "Estelle." I met Estelle while conducting a stress reduction workshop for employees at the Hebrew Home. We were in a room called the "Conservatory," where residents frequently visit with their families and each other. Although the workshop was for staff, there were a few residents who hung around and participated as well.

As I led the workshop, I noticed that one of residents, Estelle, was not only not participating, but she was also sitting there with what looked like a scowl on her face. I know that not everyone is always "up" for laughing, so I decided not to let her behavior upset me. When I asked everyone in the group to stand, Estelle remained seated and continued to scowl. I wondered at that point if she felt excluded because she couldn't stand, but then I remembered that she walked into the room unassisted. She was not wheelchair bound. As I continued to lead the workshop, all the participants were roaring with laughter, yet Estelle didn't even crack a smile.

After the session concluded, Estelle stayed seated as everyone filed out to go back to work. She then asked if she could speak to me and proceeded to apologize for not participating. She said that she loved being there and she even told me a hysterical anecdote about an interaction she had with another resident. There was actually so much joy in her; it just wasn't showing on the outside. Who knew? That day Estelle taught me a very important lesson: Never try to judge what's going on inside of someone based on his or her outward expression. It's a lesson I won't soon forget.

Because of Estelle, I also learned that I must always come from a place of curiosity rather than expectation. I must be curious about facial expressions and body language and not assume what I think the other person is feeling. (After all, you know what they say about those who assume!) Estelle helped me realize that my expectations place a box around my thinking. However, if I can be curious instead, then every behavior is welcomed and, most important, I don't get disappointed if I notice someone not participating in Laughter Club. Being curious will ultimately give me more flexibility in how I react to what's going on around me. When I expect something, then I only look for that one thing. But when I'm curious, anything goes (reminds me of a song!).

In another instance there was a female resident who would come to the weekly Laughter Club session on her floor. Each week she would sit there and continually say, "This is stupid. This is really silly." Each time she'd act up I would agree with her and respond, "Yes, it may appear to be silly." Then I'd continue to introduce the next exercise. This dialog between us continued week after week.

One week when she arrived she began with the same behavior. But then I noticed something marvelous happen. Midway through Laughter Club, as we chanted and clapped to the Ho-Ho-Ha-Ha-Ha, I watched her tap her finger against her leg to the beat. At that point I knew I made a connection – albeit a small one. Even though she wasn't going all out like the other participants, she was finally getting it! From that point on she didn't complain about the exercises being stupid or silly. She simply tapped her finger to the beat of the chant and participated in her own small way. Thanks to her I learned that even the most challenging people are reachable if you give them the time and space they need.

As a result of the work I do and the many people I interact with, I've also learned that it's important for me to stretch my boundaries from time to time. I encourage my Laughter Club laughers to do the same. However, I don't think I'd be able to do that if it weren't for a gentleman I'll call "William."

By all accounts, William is a Laughter Club heckler. Whenever I lead the group through the exercises, he playfully groans during the exhalations or puts in some verbal jabs about the various activities. Normally behavior such as William's prompts me to doubt my abilities and question my life's purpose. However, when William began acting up, I decided to take a different route. Rather than try to dissuade his behavior, I welcomed his musings and talked to the group about the "rules" of clowning, specifically that we need to dare to break the rules. I then encouraged the other group members to heckle a little and take risks to be zany.

What followed was a magnified volume of laughter as I encouraged their little mischievous internal kids to come out and play. Granted, it was risky for me to encourage that sort of behavior, but seeing how happy it made William to playfully heckle gave me the courage to take a risk myself. For the seniors, this kind of organized chaos enabled them to let go and embrace the good feelings that laughter can elicit. William helped me realize that we all need to break the rules once in a while in order to fully experience the joys life has to offer.

The Ultimate Gifts From My Special Heroes

The biggest gift of all is simply to be with someone. And being with all these older people has helped me finally realize just how young I really am. There was a time when I'd wake up and think, "Oh my God. I'm forty-nine! I'm so old." Now I wake up and think, "Oh my God. I just had my fifty-second birthday! I am so young!" And that helps me appreciate the time I have with my family and friends.

Another gift I've received is the gift of patience. Some people can be extremely difficult to connect with, and it takes a healthy dose of perseverance to get through those times. I now know that sometimes just sitting and breathing with someone is all they need to stay in the moment and be in good humor. By having the patience to be there for those people, I can get positive feedback from them and watch those connection miracles happen.

Unfortunately (or maybe fortunately), I've also learned what true loneliness looks like. When I take the time to look into the eyes of some of the residents, I can see the profound loneliness in their spirits. I also talk to staff Social Workers and hear the stories of those families who never come to visit. The other day I saw a man crying and speaking Russian as he was rolling down the hall in his wheelchair. It's during those times that I can see, hear, feel, and taste the loneliness people are feeling. These heroes have also shown me what real pain looks like, which helps me realize that the little things I sometimes feel are nothing at all.

Perhaps most important is the feeling of gratitude my heroes have helped foster within my soul. Sometimes I say that I think I've been lucky to have such wonderful experiences in life. But I really don't think it has anything to do with luck. That's why I now express my gratitude for all the "coincidences" that have guided my life. Deep down I know they're not coincidences, that every event is part of a grand plan. And so I'm grateful that I've been in this space at this point of my life.

I'm also grateful for so many things in my past that I once thought were misfortunes. In fact, those misfortunes have given me more sensitivity to be able to work with so many wonderfully amazing people. By interacting with both the residents and staff, I've learned volumes about myself, and I know these experiences have hastened my spiritual growth. And for that, to all my heroes, I simply say, "Thank you."

Chapter Six

Laugh and the World Laughs With You

"What soap is to the body, laughter is to the soul."
—Yiddish Proverb

A side from working with the residents, one of my greatest joys is working with the staff at the Hebrew Home. The Nurses and Aides I interact with are the most dedicated and amazing people I have ever met. They work for eight to ten hours daily with an array of ill people, take care of bodily fluids, and some even act as surrogate families for the residents. It's hard, thankless work, and each and every one of them deserves a medal. I sometimes wonder if I'd be able to do what they do day in and day out. Honestly, I don't think I have it in me. Their talent and dedication blow me away. I'm so grateful to work with such an amazing bunch of people.

I'm also thankful that my work at the Home benefits the staff as much as it does the residents and me. I love seeing the staffs' faces light up when I enter the unit. Even though they may be having a stressful day, whether it be because of resident or employment issues, they can't help but smile when they see Elfinya come by. I consider it a marvelous bonus to be able to brighten their day, lighten their stress load, and help them initiate some good, hearty laughter.

The more I talk with the staff, the more I realize just how desperately they need humor in their day as well. I love seeing them get involved with the Laughter Clubs and joining in with the laughter exercises. Afterwards, they tell me that they feel so much "lighter" after I visit. They laugh more for the rest of day. Their stresses don't seem so insurmountable. They smile at each other and spread laughter and joy throughout the building and to other units I'm not scheduled in. It's a trickle effect that permeates nearly every corridor and every nurse's station.

One day when I was getting ready to leave for the day, I passed by an elevator. At that precise moment the elevator doors opened and a group of nurses came out. They were all chanting Ho-Ho-Ha-Ha-Ha and doing some Laughter Club laughs. The smiles on their faces lit up the corridor. Everyone in the hallway heard them and turned to look at what was going on. Before anyone knew it, everyone within earshot was laughing. I felt such a sense of peace in the air and was thrilled to see the effects of my Laughter Clubs being passed on. The laughter was infectious, and this was one infection I was glad everyone caught!

My Favorite Clownling

I've made some wonderful friends as a result of being Elfinya, but none are as dear as my favorite clownling Irene, whose clown name is "Sunshine." I first met Irene at the hospital. She was a volunteer in the gift shop. Whenever I would come in for a visit, Irene and I would banter some funny one-liners back and forth. Irene seemed enthralled with what I was doing for the patients, and I in turn was intrigued with Irene's curiosity and abundant sense of humor. I loved visiting the gift shop to talk with her. Her spirit was so strong and felt so in-tune with my own.

One day during our usual visit, Irene asked if she could clown with me for a day. I thought, why not! I asked if she had ever clowned before; she said no. So I gave her some clowning advice and tips, offered some suggestions for a simple clown character, and made plans to have her walk around with me the following week.

That next Tuesday I met Irene at the hospital entrance for our clowning date. Since she had never clowned before, I wasn't expecting her to be completely made up. I figured she'd simply wear some bright, fun clothes and maybe carry a prop or two. When she approached the building, what I saw stopped me in my tracks.

Irene had on a neon yellow wig with curls cascading down to her shoulders. Her cheeks were painted with bright red circles and her eyes were made up in white and blue eye shadow. She drew in some fake eyebrows, making her appear as if she had a permanent surprise look on her face. She also wore a pair of denim overalls adorned with small teddy bears and bright ribbons. She looked absolutely beautiful. She looked like a ray of sunshine! The name stuck.

As we made our way through the hospital, I explained to her the concepts of Caring Clowning, caring humor, and the different types of humor. She intently observed me as I interacted with the first patient of the day – a lady suffering from Alzheimer's. The lady couldn't speak, but she seemed to recognize my face. As I sat with her and held her hand, the connection occurred. Our facial expressions and breathing were in perfect harmony. Her face lit up, and she cupped my cheek with her hand. Just then she began to giggle. I joined in, and for the next few minutes, the two of us were in our own little spiritual world.

After we left the lady, I asked Irene what she thought of the experience. She said she was amazed at how the woman seemed to "come to life." She felt the "joy and connection" that a Caring Clown and Therapeutic Humor brought to the lady. From that moment on, Irene was hooked. She slowly started interacting with the patients and using my rapport building techniques. Soon the patients knew her by name. And if Irene was unable to attend one week, I'd get bombarded with the question of the day: "Where's Sunshine?"

As the weeks turned to months, Irene became my regular Wednesday companion at the hospital. When I began working at the Hebrew Home, she accompanied me there as well, and began assisting me every Thursday as I visited the various residents. Sadly, Irene had to leave clowning to pursue other endeavors in October 2001.

I miss her.

While I'm sure I had taught Irene a lot about Therapeutic Humor, she taught me so much more in regards to my own personality and my ability to connect with others. She continually taught me how to stay in the moment and how to be more sensitive to what's really important. For example, there was one instance when a Hebrew Home volunteer came up to me and asked if she could have eight of the funny stickers I hand out after Laughter Club. She went on to explain that she had a disability and lived in a group home. She wanted the extra stickers to give to some of the people she lived with.

As soon as the lady asked for the stickers, my left brain kicked into gear. *"I can't give stickers to people who aren't here. We have a budget we have to adhere to for supplies. What if everyone else starts wanting eight extra stickers?"* The reasons not to give the lady the stickers raced through my mind. Irene, who obviously sensed this internal dialogue going on inside me, turned to me and said, "Jacki, it's only eight stickers."

My right brain then piped in and said, *"Of course. What's wrong with me? Where is my heart?"* And then I immediately handed the lady the eight stickers she requested. So on those occasions when my heart escaped me and I lost sight of what's really important, Irene was there to remind me. Thanks to Irene, I was able to not only make another person happy that day, but I also enabled her to pass that joy onto others.

Having Irene assist me at the Home was a wonderful experience. We were both teachers and students to each other.

We remain two kindred spirits totally in sync. I doubt I could have designed a more perfect relationship if I had tried.

Daily Inspiration

No two days as a Humor Therapist are the same. Each day I conduct a Laughter Club session, I notice a certain "theme" of the day. It's almost as if there's a unifying energy in the building, and whatever emotion is most prevalent for the day is what the day's theme becomes.

For instance, "sadness" is unfortunately a common theme. One day I was so touched by a man crying and speaking Russian as he was rolling down the hall in his wheel chair. I imagined that he was feeling a sense of isolation. I don't know for sure, but that's what he touched in me. That same day I was again deeply moved by a visitor who was crying because her mother's health was clearly failing. I tried to connect with the mother. It didn't work. As I sat with the grieving daughter, I felt a sense of relief that that part of my life was over. I've been there and done that with both my parents.

Another time right before I started the laughter exercises, one of the residents was very tearful. I asked her what was wrong, and she told me that she hated being there and wanted to die. I listened. She cried. I wanted to cry too. She said how lonely she was and that she desperately wanted to go home. Residents frequently tell me that they just want out.

After a few minutes, the woman said she wanted to go back to her room, and so I walked her down the hall to her room. Once inside, I helped her into a chair by her window. She didn't want to talk anymore and asked to be left alone. I honored her request. I left her room and walked back to where the Laughter Club session was being held. I felt sad and wondered how I was going to laugh when I'd just been saturated with so much pain.

When I arrived at the meeting spot, fifteen residents were waiting for the fun to begin. I pulled myself together – I had no choice. I started with the breathing, and almost immediately everyone was raising and lowering their hands as they inhaled and exhaled. Then we went on to Ho-Ho-Ha-Ha-Ha! They loved it. We then began some other Laughter Club exercises and I felt so much better. Interacting with the residents energized my spirit all over again. That experience was yet another reminder that Laughter Club is medicine for me too.

Did Laughter Club take away my sadness that day? Yes…for a little while. Did I still feel sad afterwards? Yes. Did I get a welcomed respite from my yuckiness? Absolutely! Did it reaffirm my love for this work? YYEESSS! I realized once again that day that my humor is a gift and that it's a privilege to be on the giving and receiving side of it. Those challenging experiences deepen my resolve to continue to give these folks a respite from their pain.

Fortunately, another common theme is "gratitude." So often the residents thank me and thank me some more for conducting the Laughter Club sessions. I want so much to make a difference. On those days when I see, hear, and feel that gratitude, I know in the core of my core that I am doing just that. Laughter Clubs are powerful vehicles in which to make that difference. Hearing someone tell me, "Thank you. You've helped me forget the pain for a few moments," makes up for all the sadness.

Of all the so-called "themes," "playfulness" is by far my favorite. I love when I can get the residents acting like kids again. In June 2000, the Hebrew Home held a combination Mother's Day and Father's Day celebration. I was scheduled to work that day, so I made an appearance in the Social Hall, where the event was being held. I went dressed in my cowgirl outfit, a.k.a. Bed Pannie Oakley. I wore black jeans, a black vest, and a bedpan for a hat. I also brought my stick horse "Stewball." He's a very special stick horse because if you press a certain place on his head, he makes clopping sounds, then he nays, and finally he lets out a loud horse snort. I absolutely love it!

When I made my appearance in the Social Hall, I felt especially playful that day, so I romped around the room with Stewball like a five-year-old. Guess what? The residents loved the playfulness as well. I held Stewball up to their ears so they could hear the sounds. The sillier I got, the more they laughed. When that playful spirit takes over, I feel like I'm in heaven…Home.

On another instance I went to the Home dressed as Elfinya. I visited the end stage Alzheimer's and Dementia unit and blew bubbles with the residents. I know I connected with at least five or six of the most compromised residents. They delighted in my clown character as well as the bubbles. The more bubbles I blew, the more they reached for them and laughed. Some especially liked the feeling when the bubble popped on their hand. Even though these people's brains and bodies could no longer play, their spirits were very much alive. It was almost as if someone had said, "Can 'Susie' come out and play?"

After that day, I decided I wanted to play more with the staff. I noticed how tired they looked, and I wanted that playfulness essence to rub off on them too. So on my next visit I brought my "wiggly, giggly" ball, which makes funny noises when you shake or throw it. When I appeared at the nurse's station, some of them were eager for a break, while others claimed they had no time to play. I told them that if they took a short play break they'd be able to work more efficiently for the rest of the day. Some of them played and felt better; some of them chose not to play. That's okay. I can only give people what they're willing to receive.

When I first brought the ball, I thought it would be primarily for the staff. Boy, was I wrong! The residents in the early Alzheimer's unit wanted to play ball too. Who am I to say no to some good fun? We played for nearly an hour. The residents loved the sounds the ball made and the interaction. One of the residents even came up to me and told me how beautiful I was as Elfinya. I loved it! But then again, who wouldn't? One resident, who was slumped over in her wheelchair, chose not to play ball. When I sat next to her to make a connection, magic occurred. She looked up at me and said, "Smile. You're on Candid Camera!" My spirit was absolutely soaring! Rock and Roll!

The Dance

There is one resident at the Hebrew Home (I'll call her "Anne") who is eighty-something years old and who spends a great deal of time "walking" the halls in her wheel chair. She has snow-white hair that is usually pulled back into a ponytail. As she rides around the units, she is often stooped over.

The staff originally told me that Anne spoke Russian, but as I spent more time with her, I realized that she spoke Yiddish too. Because we don't speak the same language, my interactions with her are truly a case of demonstrating that humor transcends language. As I mentioned earlier, in order to establish rapport with people, it's helpful to be in relatively the same body position as the person with whom I am interacting. So, whenever I interact with Anne, I find an extra wheelchair and "walk" the halls with her.

Our "walks" aren't the usual type of walk, however. Those who observe us say it looks more like a dance. As Anne makes her way down the hall, she uses her feet to propel her wheelchair. She keeps the palms of her hands together, almost in a praying position, and lets them "swim" through the air. Left to right and up and down, her hands glide through the air as her wheelchair effortlessly floats down the hall. I, of course, mirror her actions, so the two of us are like dance partners moving in perfect harmony and synchronicity.

Although I've spent approximately a half hour per week with her for nearly a year, I was never absolutely certain whether or not Anne recognized me. One day I was in the Activities Office talking with one of the therapists who is fluent in Russian.

I was trying to learn a few words so I could connect with Anne. Who should happen to roll by at that precise moment? Anne! Upon seeing me, she turned her wheelchair around and rolled into the office. She reached out to me, smiled loudly, opened her arms, and embraced me with the most delicious hug! I melted, and of course, responded in kind.

I then spent the next half hour "walking" the halls with her. During that half hour, she would extend her hand and take mine. Sometimes she would cry. When she would cry, I would stop my wheelchair and she hers, and she would reach out to me and cradle her head in my chest. We would then breathe in unison. Then she would stop and we would "walk" together a little more, the whole time with her talking in a combination of Russian and Yiddish non-stop. The next thing I knew, she would begin laughing, and we would laugh together.

Can you imagine what it looks like to see a clown "walking" and "dancing" in a wheelchair side by side with this beautiful woman? The staff gets a kick out of seeing me ride around in the wheelchair, and so it is a break for them as well. Moments like this confirm the fact that I love my job. I also love Anne even though we don't speak the same language. Being with Anne and seeing her willingly interact with me puts the "aah" in my "ha."

Reaching Out

In July 2001, the HA!HA!LOGY bug spread again. I was asked to visit another assisted living center in the Washington DC area and conduct a Laughter Club session for the residents. Of course I said yes. The events that followed gave me new inspiration to keep going.

On the morning of July 18, 2001 I got dressed in my clown costume and headed out. I was less than an hour away but I decided to give myself at least an hour and a half to get there. I wasn't exactly sure where the house was, it was raining that day, and I always get anxious when I have to travel to a new place all alone.

The rain that day actually made me happy because it gave me a chance to use my favorite umbrella. When opened, the umbrella looks like one of the monsters from Maurice Sendak's *Where the Wild Things Are*, complete with monster ears. I always get stares when I use that umbrella – even more so when I use it dressed as Elfinya.

As I entered the facility, I noticed what a beautiful building it was. The house was a remodeled private residence. Antique furniture and elaborate artwork adorned the lobby. I approached the first resident I saw and offered a cheerful "Hello." He looked at me and said nothing. "Uh-oh," I thought.

I then walked to the receptionist counter. The receptionist took one look at me and squealed, "Ooooooh! We've been expecting you." (One side benefit of being dressed as a clown is that you rarely have to introduce yourself.) I sighed out of relief upon seeing his excitement.

He led me to the room where I would be conducting the Laughter Club. Several residents were already present. As I set up the room, more and more residents trickled in. By the start time, I had an audience of 20 people. I offered my usual, cheery, "Morning!" and got a wonderful response. It was clear that these folks very much wanted to laugh.

As we went through the Laughter Club exercises, there were many opportunities for ad-libbing and improvisation. I was in my element. The session lasted for 45 minutes. Since I was scheduled to be there for an hour, I asked the Activities Director if I could go up on the floors for some one-on-one interaction. She said yes.

Once upstairs, one of the nurses asked if I would visit one of her patients who was dying. I agreed and downshifted into my slowest gear. When I reached the patient's room, I peeked around the corner and asked if it was okay that I enter. The lady inside said yes. I was expecting to see someone in a vegetative state, but what I saw was a wonderful woman lying in bed who was eager to meet me.

The woman's face was so animated that I found it hard to believe she was dying. Apparently, her illness was so far advanced that her family and the staff were literally waiting for her to take her last breath.

The woman spoke to me and told me her name: "Maureen." She then reached out to me and began playing with the props on my clown costume. I asked if I could give her a "bubble bath" (my term for blowing bubbles and showering them on people). She agreed and played with the bubbles I blew her way. As the bubbles popped on her face and hands, Maureen and I connected and shared some moments of giggling. Even though she was dying, she seemed so free as she bathed in the bubbles.

After I left the room, the nurse on duty approached me and thanked me for visiting Maureen. She said that Maureen was unresponsive the last few days, and she was grateful that I was able to evoke some positive response from her. As we rode down on the elevator together, the nurse continued to thank me, and then she began to cry. She told me what a blessing I was and what a gift I had brought to her patient. I thanked her for her kind words and said good-bye.

Before I left the facility, the Activities Director stopped me and asked if I could come back in August, September, and October. I was delighted. Her repeat invitation yet again confirmed my gift and the fact that I am making a difference in the lives of people. I left the building that day thinking that I couldn't wait to go back there the following month. **Aaaaaaaaaaaah!**

New Perspectives

Working at the Hebrew Home is truly a joy. It's a wonderful spiritual homecoming for me. Because I have so much history with the Hebrew Home and have denied my Jewishness for so much of my life, it feels good to "come home" again. Bubbe (my grandmother) lived at the Hebrew Home when it was on

Spring Road. My Aunt Anne worked there, then she and Aunt Jennie lived at the Home when it moved to Rockville. I have a cousin who resides at the Home now. I make it a point to see her at least every two weeks.

One thing is for certain: being a Humor Therapist is such a roller coaster ride. There are many ups and downs every day. For instance, I may go to a unit and only connect with a couple of people there. My first instinct is to say, "How awful. I only connected with two people." However, I know that I must look at everything in a positive way and say instead, "Hooray! I connected with two people today!" I know that each life is special and making even the smallest connection with just one person is a great accomplishment.

As I roam the halls of the Hebrew Home, I often wonder if one day I'll wind up in a place like this. I like to think that I'll always be healthy enough to take care of myself, but I can't predict the future. All I do know is that as long as I can find a way to laugh, I can overcome and persevere through any challenge that comes my way.

Chapter Seven

The Heart and Soul of Laughter

"At the height of laughter, the universe is flung into a kaleidoscope of new possibilities." - Jean Houston

There's no doubt about it: Spreading joy and laughter is my life's calling. Another part of my mission is to teach others about the concepts of Caring Clowning and encourage them to spread laughter as well. That's why one of my most profound experiences was teaching teenage kids what Caring Clowning is all about.

When I first started volunteering at the hospital, a group of high school juniors and seniors approached me. They were regular volunteers at the hospital and heard about my HA!HA!LOGY program. They said that they had recently seen the movie *Patch Adams* and they wanted to learn more about Caring Clowning and Humor Therapy. I had never taught teenagers before, so I figured this would be a great learning experience for both the kids and me.

I proceeded to create a six-week course for these juniors and seniors. We met once a week at the hospital for Humor Therapy 101. We talked about infection control, rapport building techniques, how to create a clown character, how to work with puppets and props, how to apply clown makeup, and a host of other topics I had learned at Clown Camp. At the end of the six weeks, I allowed them to clown with me on the floors. My new bunch of clownlings was hatched!

The patients loved the junior clowns. As the kids interacted with the patients, they received all sorts of thanks and positive feedback. One elderly man kissed one of the little female clownlings on the head. She cried the rest of the afternoon.

Watching these kids get in touch with their sensitive side was a truly rewarding experience. These days, it appears that a lot of older kids are cynical. They're obsessed with what is "cool" and what is not. In a matter of a few weeks, these kids learned that helping others is indeed a cool thing to do.

Because of the apparent success of this experience, a middle school teacher approached me and asked if I would do a course on Caring Clowning for some twelve and thirteen year olds. The idea of teaching middle school kids terrified me, as I'm not a very good disciplinarian. Sure, I raised two of my own children, but disciplining someone else's kids in a classroom setting is a totally different ballgame. I struggled with this decision for a long time. On one hand, I thought it would be great to introduce a younger group of children to Caring Clowning. On the other hand, I knew that twelve and thirteen year olds were still in the "I hate boys" and "I hate girls" phase. I anticipated them to be throwing things at each other and making faces across the room the entire time. Ultimately, the sensitive side of me won and I agreed to teach the class…with a couple of conditions.

First, I wanted the Project Director to meet with me and help me create a lesson plan for kids at this level. And two, I wanted someone who taught middle school to be in the room with me to help with any disciplinary problems. With all the conditions in place, we were ready to go. I taught the kids the same concepts as I taught the older kids, only I brought the lessons down to their level. At the end of the course, the kids were still too frightened to clown in a nursing home or hospital, so we went to an independent living home instead.

What was most amazing to me was watching these kids – boys and girls – put aside their differences and actually help each other with costumes and makeup. They seemed to grow up in a matter of moments. As they helped each other, their childish tendencies faded away, and they displayed their future mature selves. Seeing them dressed up and interacting with the residents put a warm glow in my heart. After interacting with the residents, the kids were really getting into clowning, so I suggested we do a little street clowning. The kids loved the idea.

It just so happened that in a couple of weeks there was to be a Purim Carnival going on at their Synagogue. This carnival is a celebration for the Jewish holiday of Purim where kids dress up as a variety of different biblical characters. "My kids" were clowns (not very prevalent in any Bible version I've ever read), but we decided to go anyway. They happily clowned for all the carnival participants, and they received great feedback. It was such an enriching experience for them, as it taught them about sensitivity, honoring another person's feelings, and working together as a team. Being able to connect with these kids and impact their life in a positive way was definitely one of the highlights of my career. I only hope that they can carry these lessons on into their teenage and adult years.

The Learned Fear of Laughter

Unfortunately, laughing and clowning around are problematic issues for many adults. They're very self-conscious of what others think of them and are unable to let go and have a good laugh. Some will even go so far as to back away from a group of people who are laughing hysterically. I find that I react quite the opposite. When I notice a group of people laughing and having fun, I want to be with them and will do whatever I can to become included in the fun.

I believe that during our growing up years we hear a number of messages from parents and teachers that laughing is not the proper thing to do. Think about your own childhood. How many times did you hear phrases like, "This is not a laughing matter young man/lady," "If you don't stop that laughing right now you'll be standing in the corner for the rest of day," and "Would you mind sharing what's so funny with the rest of us?" As we grow up, these messages stay with us. We then pass them down to our own children and become very restrained and fearful of laughing. How sad.

While it's true that laughing publicly can sometimes be risky (depending on the situation), when you take that initial risk you find that the next one is easier. It's simply a matter of saying to yourself, "This is worth it. Laughing will make me feel better." And if people look at you strangely for having a good time, let 'em! Realize there will always be people who choose not to laugh. They choose not to see the humor in a situation. I feel sad for those people who are afraid to laugh, yet I realize they're at the place they need to be. I've learned long ago that I can't teach people to be funny. All I can do is give them permission to laugh.

Finding humor in a situation is a matter of allowing that little childlike part of yourself to come out and play. Regardless of how you perceive yourself, you do have a childlike essence within. We all do. Some people are just more comfortable letting it show than others. In today's fast-paced, bottom line oriented world, it's easy to understand why the inner child gets squashed. So many people are so filled with stress, anger, and frustration that that's what comes out. However, if people can put more laughter in their lives, then that's what the heart will hear and what the body will display. So in essence, laughing can help us all achieve a greater sense of inner peace. When that occurs, we'll feel more at ease around others and more willing to connect with total strangers.

Unfortunately, too many people are disconnected these days. Even with all the technology – the e-mail, the faxes, the voice mail, the virtual assistants, etc. – we can't keep spiritually connected. We've lost that face-to-face communication. We've lost the human touch to relationships. Laughter is a wonderful way to reclaim our connectedness and embrace the spirituality of relationships. Sharing humor brings down barriers, frees the soul, and allows the spiritual interaction to occur. This spiritual connection that transpires is not mystical or even religious. It's the essence of our humanity – our inherent need to develop meaningful relationships and to love and be loved. Laughter, happiness, humor, and joy are at the root of that essence. So denying it is denying who we are, while embracing it is following the Universe's natural plan. The choice is totally yours.

Laughing Imagery

Using imagery is a wonderful way to get into a more positive state of mind. It's almost like a form of meditation where you attempt to clear your mind and direct your focus to a more uplifting place. By calming your mind and releasing your stress, you allow laughter the opportunity to bubble up. It's a spiritual cleansing process that opens you up to the humor that's around you daily.

Since many people are not familiar with imagery or meditation (they envision Monks in a Monastery or Yogis bent in some awkward position), I have developed a Laughing Exercise that can assist you with getting into a more positive state of mind. By practicing this exercise daily, you can free your spirit and invite humor into your life.

Before you create this image in your mind, check with your healthcare provider to make sure you are free from any pre-existing conditions that may prevent you from receiving the full benefit of this exercise. For more information about Guided Imagery, refer to the book *Staying Well With Guided Imagery* by Belleruth Naparstek (New York: Warner Books, Inc. 1994).

Imagery for Positive Humor

First, relax in a comfortable position, preferably in a place where you are fully supported. Shift your body so you feel centered. You may wish to close your eyes, or not; it's completely up to you.

Next, take a slow, deep breath…It may be helpful to make your exhale longer than your inhale. Take another breath…and another…each time visualizing your breath as a white, warm, wispy, waft of fresh air that winds its way to all parts of your body.

Focus on your breathing…Imagine that with every inhalation you take in well being, and that with every exhalation you release tension…Keep your focus on your breath. If other thoughts float by, that's okay; simply return your attention to your breath.

Now, think of a pleasing place from your past…If you can't recall one, you might try creating one. Note any special colors… special tastes… special smells… special textures… special feelings. Are you at the beach?…The mountains?…At home?…Perhaps you are with a special person?…Or maybe you are alone. It doesn't really matter as long as the experience is a pleasant one.

Is there music playing, or is it quiet?…Is the wind blowing, or is it still?…Maybe you are beside a quiet lake.

Try to notice the smells…Is there apple pie or bread baking in the oven?…Do you taste the sweet salt of the ocean?…The rain of the forest?…Can you taste some comfort food? **Yummmmmmmmmm.**

Maybe you can even feel the sand or the softness of flannel PJs after they've been worn a couple of times…Or perhaps you can feel the warmth of a fire in the fireplace…
Allow yourself to soak up all this wonderfulness of a safe and nurturing place.

Can you see someone, or maybe yourself, beginning to smile?…Imagine the corners of the lips beginning to rise…Visualize the twinkle in the eye and the eyebrows lifting…Feel the "tee-hee" coming and guide it into a hearty belly laugh…Allow your whole body to experience this most delicious dance and release.

Perhaps you hear laughter coming from this place…Do you see another favorite person?…Can you imagine the warmth and connection you feel towards this person?… Become aware of your capacity for joy…This may take some time, and that's okay.

And now…When you're ready, slowly become aware of where you are, whether you're seated in your chair or couch or lying in your bed…Become aware of your breath and the room that you're in.

As you become fully aware of your actual surroundings, know that whenever you want you can revisit the wonderful place in your mind.

Feel the aaaaaaaaah, and slowly and gently open your eyes. Feel the smile in your heart. **Aaaaaaaaaah… and… haaaaaaaaaa.** You may want to recite this exercise into a tape recorder so you can hear your own voice as a guide.

May you wear this image well!

A Life-Changing Journey

I sometimes wonder why I chose nursing homes and hospitals as my vehicle for spreading humor. After all, nursing homes and hospitals are frequently very lonely and scary places – the last place anyone would expect humor to be present. I have to think that my reason for this sort of environment stems from my childhood. One incident in particular stands out in my memory.

When I was ten years old, my parents sent me to sleep away camp for eight weeks during the summer in the tiny town of Oakland, Maine. I went every year and I always loved it. Being away from home and out in nature was so liberating. This particular summer, however, I developed boils on the inside of my thigh. The camp doctor couldn't figure out a cause and he treated the boils the best way he was able with his limited facilities. Unfortunately, the boils kept getting worse. The camp doctor finally sent me to the local hospital for treatment.

The hospital doctor who examined me decided I would need surgery to heal the boils. He explained that they would put me to sleep, cut the boils open, and let them drain. Being only ten years old, the whole process sounded absolutely horrifying. I asked the camp counselor present to please call my parents so they could be with me.

After my parents spoke to the hospital doctor, they consented to the surgery, but they never came to Maine. They were too busy in their jobs and couldn't afford to take the time off. So here I was with some camp nurse, whom I didn't know at all, in a very remote part of the country, needing surgery. As they put me under the anesthesia (which at the time was ether), I remember feeling terribly alone and terrified. I didn't fully understand what was going on, and I so desperately wanted the comfort of Mom or Dad.

I'm not revealing this incident from my past to get sympathy. I simply think that going through a traumatic experience like that instilled some feelings of fear and loneliness in me that I never forgot. As a result, I think that today I can better identify with people who are frightened and alone and can connect with them on a spiritual level.

The benefit is that as I brighten the lives of others who are lonely and scared, my feelings of isolation and fear dissipate as well. The more I work with the nursing home residents, the more in tune I feel with my own spirituality and humanity. As I make a difference in the lives of others, I make a difference in my own life as well. For example, the depression I battled for so long is greatly lessened today. The fear I felt for my entire life – fear of my parents, fear of the alcoholic maid, fear of not choosing the right career path – is a distant memory. When I'm spreading humor, my fear is gone. My spirit is free to be me. That creative, whimsical part of myself that I had to hide for so long can come out and play and embrace the world. By doing this kind of work, by bringing humor to others, by connecting with people and encouraging them to connect with each other, my fears are gone and my spirit soars.

For the first time in my life I can honestly say that I feel truly alive and happy. I feel good about the person I see in the mirror every day. I know many people can't say that about themselves, and that fact saddens me too. I would like to give as many people as possible the ability to see humor in themselves and in life so that they can feel a sense of inner peace and connectedness. I believe that every person on Earth has the capacity to be funny, and I want to unleash that ability in all so that they can start on the path to self-healing. I guess you could say that I want to heal the world "one HA at a time."

One of the Hebrew Home residents recently said to me, "If you don't have humor, you don't have life." I believe that phrase sums it up perfectly. So frequently the humor part of people's spirit atrophies, especially for people in nursing homes and hospitals. When they don't use their humor, they lose it. So I want to be able to impact people with not only the "ha-ha," but also with the "ah." I want people to be able to recognize their own life's catastrophes and self-limiting beliefs so they can use humor to heal their mind, body, and soul. It's an all-consuming personal mission, and the good news is that the work will never be completely done. The pursuit is an ongoing mission that others can join in with and reap the wonderful rewards.

The Positive Effects of Humor Can Inspire You Too

All the personal and spiritual benefits I receive as a result of being a Humor Therapist are not unique to the profession. Anyone can bring good humor to another and feel the positive emotions that I do. This does not mean that you have to dress like a clown and visit nursing homes and hospitals, or even clown in your neighborhood streets. Spreading laughter to others and forming connections can happen every day in the most common of occurrences.

Smiling to a stranger, saying "hi" to someone who looks lonely, being patient with the person in front of you in the grocery store line – all these are simple ways to spread positive humor to others. Remember, humor is not always about jokes and being silly. Sometimes it's about comforting another, "being there" for someone, and offering hope when none seems to exist. These are the things that help take people from a place of negativity and transfer them to a place filled with positive energy. When you can do this for another, you transcend any existing or perceived barrier and you form a meaningful connection with the other person. You then have the basis for a spiritual relationship and can receive the benefits that are inherent in helping another.

The whole aspect of positive humor reminds me of a column Ann Landers printed a few years ago. I thought the column was so fitting to my message that I cut it out and saved it. I read it whenever I am feeling down or questioning my life's work. The message is titled, "What Cancer Cannot Do." It reads: "Cancer is so limited. It cannot cripple love. It cannot shatter hope. It cannot corrode faith. It cannot destroy peace. It cannot kill friendship. It cannot suppress memories. It cannot silence courage. It cannot invade the soul. It cannot steal eternal life. It cannot conquer the spirit."

All the mentioned elements in the piece are the exact ones that humor touches. In fact, you can substitute Cancer with Alzheimer's, Arthritis, or any other kind of limitation. However, whatever is disabling you or someone you know can't destroy the things that humor impacts. So as you go out and spread joy to others, always remember that positive humor is about embracing love, hope, faith, peace, friendship, memories, courage, soul, and eternal life. All these elements are an intrinsic part of your spirit and are what positive humor is all about.

Chapter Eight

The Path of Humor Leads to Home

"We become so overwhelmed by illness, death, and grief that we forget that humor, like the moon, can bring relief to our darkest times."–Allen Klein

The Dalai Lama once said, "I love smiles and laughter." Me too! Like most people, I want more smiles and laughter in my life, and I'm always on the lookout for ways to create the right conditions for it. What the Dalai Lama said is both in my heart and in the spirit of the Laughter Clubs. As a Therapeutic Clown and Laughter Club Leader, I have embraced this most delicious union. I now invite you to do the same!

While I don't expect everyone who reads this to become a Caring Clown or lead Laughter Clubs, I do hope you to do little things to bring laughter into your life each and every day. So often people tell me, "Jacki, I love what you do and I desperately want to bring more humor into my life. But my life is so stressful. How can I possibly take the time for laughter?"

I always tell these people that there are plenty of small and simple ways to add humor to your life. The following chart should help stimulate some ideas for your own circumstances.

Easy Ways to Improve Your Sense of Humor

- Watch a funny video
- Listen to a humorous audiotape while driving to work
- Get some funny props - a clown nose, an outrageous wig, a rubber chicken...anything that will encourage laughter in yourself and others
- Read the comics
- Move your body (changing your physiology changes your emotional state)
- Hang out with a kid
- Attend a humor workshop or a Laughter Club session
- Give yourself permission to make mistakes...and then learn from them and laugh about them
- Last and oh so very important, as Dr. Kataria has titled his book, "Laugh For No Reason"

As you bring humor into your life, realize that there may be times when humor is not appropriate. For example, if you're in the middle of a crisis, it's often difficult to step back and see the event from a different perspective. However, when you make positive humor a part of your daily life, you will develop the perspective you need to be able to disconnect from the event a little bit. Some time may need to pass, though, if the trauma is severe. Then you'll be able to face the trauma with a renewed sense of solidarity and perseverance. You'll realize that nothing is insurmountable as long as you can keep your attitude positive and not give in to the negative stuff.

I see such transformations happen every day at the nursing homes and assisted living facilities I visit. In fact, bringing positive humor and fun to these folks is the most rewarding form of therapy I've ever facilitated. This is what I've personally noticed:

1. There can be joy in an often joyless setting for the residents who are bored, depressed, and lonely AND for the staff who are often unsung heroes and angels.
2. Residents with Parkinson's disease often have fewer tremors while doing the laughter exercises.
3. The residents connect with each other through laughter and interact more after the session is over.
4. Residents have improved coordination.
5. Some of the residents with Alzheimer's disease remember the exercises from week to week.

I'm not the only one who recognizes these occurrences. Laughter Club leaders in long-term care facilities across the country echo my observations. And if people whose bodies are severely compromised can receive such positive benefits, imagine the awesome benefits available to all! Don't wait! Laugh now!

Childlike Laughter

I also want to urge everyone to help children develop a positive sense of humor that they can carry with them into adulthood. So often adults inadvertently squash the fun, whimsical essence of childhood because they want their children to be more "mature." I believe true maturity is being able to see the humor and wonder in everyday situations.

One day while I was cleaning out my attic, I found a box of my old school papers. In it were some report cards from my pre-school days (age 3). As I reviewed them, I realized just how early in life patterns of behavior are established. For example, on all those early report cards I scored low in "self-esteem" but high in "play" categories. Those comments rang true in my older years when I thought less of myself and only wanted to play and joke around. I believe I was "playing" out that evaluation.

What caught my eye on the report cards, however, was a category called "Social Attitudes and Social Behavior." Under that main category was the subcategory of "Humor." The teacher had the option of choosing one of three descriptions to rate me. They were:

1. Spontaneous; eager to enjoy and share humorous situations.
2. Sees humor in situations when attention is called to it.
3. Slow in responding to humorous situations.

All three of the pre-school report cards had option one checked. So even way back at age three I had a remarkable sense of humor. Some things never change!

Sometimes I wonder if a sense of humor is hereditary. I thought about this a lot after my father died. Shortly after his death, I went to his apartment to clean it out. As I went through his nightstand, I found a wad of papers rubber-banded together. In it were sheets and sheets of jokes that he had handwritten. Now, my dad liked to tell jokes. This was the same man who sent me from the dinner table for laughing? As I read some of his jokes, I realized that in the core of his core he must have loved to laugh. He also must have passed that torch on to me, because no matter how much trouble I got into for being funny, I still continued to do it.

Unlike my dad, though, I don't do jokes. I'm one of those people who always forgets the punch line. I'm much better at improv and finding humor in the moment. Despite our differences, finding that pack of jokes buried in my dad's nightstand was a grounding experience for me. I realized at that moment just how much alike we really were. I still have his handwritten jokes. I haven't read them all; I save them for my darkest moments and use them to lift my spirit when nothing else seems to work. Reading each one of his jokes is like having my dad by my side and cheering me on. I only wish he would have been so supportive of my sense of humor while he was living.

Lessons From a Clown

One of the most wonderful things about being a clown is that clowns are supposed to make mistakes. In fact, the more I think about it, the more I realize that in some respects, clowns are more human than humans. Humans make mistakes – period. So many people never allow themselves to make mistakes. If they do make a mistake, they emotionally beat themselves up by saying things like, "I'm so stupid. How could I do that!" or "What was I thinking? I must be an idiot!" How sad to deny yourself such a wonderful learning and laughing experience.

How wonderful that clowns are expected to make mistakes! That's one reason why people laugh at clowns. It's a big part of why being a Therapeutic Clown is so freeing. It allows me the opportunity to release the childlike essence of myself that I had to so often hide.

As I mentioned earlier, I grew up in a setting where I was expected to be a little grown-up. Whenever I made a mistake, my parents acted like it was the end of the universe. For instance, if I spilled milk at the dinner table, my parents and housekeeper would yell at me for wasting milk or ruining the table. But think about it. What's more important? The spilled milk that cost maybe five cents per glass or a child's self-image? Very often in my childhood the milk was more important. And so I love being a clown now because clowns are supposed to make mistakes and spill milk and act silly. All those moments are so very human. The more I clown, the more forgiving I become of myself and others. That's a precious gift.

All this reminds me of a story I once read in one of the *Chicken Soup* books about a scientist who was being interviewed about his work. When asked what gave him the perseverance to keep going back in the lab after the formula failed time and time again, the scientist said that he owed his internal drive and curious nature to his mom.

He went on to explain that he grew up during the time when the milkman delivered milk to the house. The milk came in big, heavy glass bottles with cardboard stoppers that were insecure. The bottles were hard to handle and easy to drop. The rule in his house was that he couldn't get his own milk from the icebox because his mother was sure he would drop the heavy bottle.

One day, being the curious and headstrong young boy that he was, he decided to get his own milk anyway. So he went to the icebox, pulled out the bottle, and just as his mother always feared, he dropped it. The milk went everywhere. His mom, who was in the next room, heard the commotion and came running in. When she saw what had happened, she didn't yell or berate her son. Instead, she said, "Wow! What a wonderful mess you've made. Life gets messy at times. Since the mess is here, we might as well play in it for a while."

So the two began to play in the spilled milk. They got on their hands and knees and splatted the milk with their hands. Then they pulled their fingers through the various milk puddles and made all sorts of funny patterns. After a half hour of this play, the milk began to get sticky, so they decided to clean it up. The boy wiped up the milk with a rag while his mother mopped the floor behind him.

Once everything was clean, his mother said, "Since you spilled the milk, I'm going to teach you how to carry the bottle so you don't spill it in the future." She then demonstrated how to hold the bottle with one hand under the bottom and the other around the bottle's neck. She led her son outside to practice carrying the empty bottle. After he mastered that feat, she filled the bottle with water so he could practice carrying it full. Before long the boy knew how to carry and maneuver the bottle to pour his own milk.

The scientist said that day his mother taught him the importance of learning from mistakes and that we shouldn't give up because of one failure. Without her continual guidance and patience, he may never have achieved so much in his adult life.

After I read that story, I thought to myself, "M-a-a-a-n! If only all parents could be so nurturing and supportive of their children. Imagine what a wonderful future we'd be creating for ourselves." I was so glad that I read that story while my own children were still living at home. Not only did it teach me that I shouldn't get upset over small mishaps, but it also helped me realize that I needed to find the perfection in our human imperfections and not take life so seriously. What a very "clowny" ideal!

Visions of Home

Do I think that humor can solve all the world's problems? Of course not. I do believe, though, that being in good humor can give us the resolve and positive mindset we need to face our challenges head on. As comedian Bill Cosby once said, "If you can find humor in anything, you can survive it."

All my experiences have proven to me that humor can unite people on a level that goes beyond the physical realm. The simple act of laughing creates a connection that can't be seen, but that can be felt at our very core. Laughing releases our spirit from our physical body and enables it to touch another, learn from that person, and grow to be the best we can possibly be. The more we allow ourselves to laugh and to find the humor in everyday events, the greater our spiritual awakening will be. That's why it's imperative for each person to find the humor in his or her life and make those positive humor connections with others.

Each day I work as a Humor Therapist I get one step closer to "home," that place where my spirit can be eternally free and content. My wish is that everyone can one day feel the essence of "home" in their own life. I want everyone to experience the joys of discovering their own spirituality through humor so that they can feel the "ah" that's inherent in every "ha."

Embracing my own spirituality, working in an environment that personifies my Jewish upbringing, and feeling more alive and in-tune with myself than ever before are all important steps of my homeward bound journey. As I continue to travel along this path and master the lessons I'm destined to learn, I feel more at peace with myself. Each step I take brings me closer to my white light and intensifies the warmth that permeates my soul. As long as those feelings keep getting stronger, I'll know that I'm on the right path.

When I finally do reach the threshold of "home," I'm confident that I'll be ready to open the door and enter. And no matter how wonderful and amazing this journey becomes, I know that "home" is not my ending destination. For me, it's just the beginning.

Jacki

Appendix

Are you or is someone you know in an assisted living or nursing home? Would you like to add more humor to such an environment? Here's how you can get a Therapeutic Humor program started in a facility near you.

1. Begin as a volunteer or friendly visitor by making weekly visits to area nursing homes. This allows you to get to know the workings of a particular facility. Bring with you some funny props, stickers, cartoons, and buttons to pin onto your volunteer jacket. If the facility will allow puppets, bring them too. I've found some great humorous stickers at Bubba's Clown Supply Shop (www.bubbasikes.com). Allow the residents to interact with you at their convenience. Remember, not everyone is up for humor. Allow them to proceed at their own pace. The longer you volunteer, the better the staff will get to know you.

2. If the feedback you receive from your weekly visits is positive, talk to the home's Director of Activities or Director of Social Work. Tell them that there are Humor Therapy programs going on around the country that are beneficial for not only the residents, but also the staff.

3. Write a proposal to initiate the Humor Therapy program. Appendix B contains a copy of the proposal I wrote to the local hospital when I was first developing HA!HA!LOGY. As you read the proposal, note the humor I interjected throughout. A very valuable workshop I attended while at The HUMOR Project talked about incorporating little

bits of humor into potentially serious documents. So when I created my proposal, I took the liberty to make the proposal a little less dry. When you create your proposal, know that it's okay to add levity to a serious correspondence.

4. Share this book with others so they can learn about the power of humor. Also, read and recommend the books listed in Appendix D.

5. Get some training in the area of Therapeutic Humor. If you want to be a Caring Clown, for example, there are a number of Clown Schools throughout the United States and the world. The one I went to was Clown Camp at the University of Wisconsin, LaCrosse. Go to www.caoi.org for more information about locating a "clown alley" in your geographic location. Try to find one that is specifically for Caring Clowns.

6. Attend workshops provided by The HUMOR Project in Saratoga Springs, NY or by the Association for Applied and Therapeutic Humor. Through these organizations you can learn how you can apply the concepts of Therapeutic Humor into your life, the lives of those you love, and a myriad of workplaces.

7. Begin to experiment and learn how you work with people. A good deal of setting up a Humor Therapy program involves experimentation and seeing what works. It reminds me of a well-known insurance company who advertises its motto: "The greatest risk is not taking one." That same motto could apply to setting up a Humor Therapy program. Tackling such an endeavor may seem like a

big risk, but if you don't risk and don't do it, you can never win.

8. Use your imagination – the options are endless!

9. Call, fax, or e-mail me for more information about setting up a Humor Therapy program in your area. I would be happy to consult with your organization to help you get started.
   Jacki@hahalogy.com
   www.hahalogy.com
   Phone: 301-907-4610
   Fax: 301-907-4610

Proposal for the Development of the Division of
HA!HA!LOGY®

The connection between humor and healing has been
explored for thousands of years.

" A merry heart doeth good like a medicine."
The Bible

*"Humor, more than anything else in the human makeup,
affords an aloofness and an ability to rise above any
situation, even if only for a few seconds."*
Victor Frankl

I am proposing the creation of a hospital-wide
Therapeutic Humor Program. Since there are already the
departments of Oncology, Radiology, Pathology, etc., I am
suggesting that this be called the "Division of HA!HA!LOGY."
The model for this program is based on a model developed by
Leslie Gibson, RN, BS, at Morton Plant Hospital in Clearwater,
Florida.

Therapeutic Humor may be defined as any positive
encounter that connects the mind and body through cognition,
emotions, and spirituality to promote healing.

The purpose of the Division of HA!HA!LOGY is to be
an adjunct to medical treatment and nursing care with the goal
of stress reduction and increased resistance to disease. Lee S.
Berk, Dr.PH, and Stanley Tan, M.D., at the Loma Linda
University School of Medicine have documented their research
demonstrating the positive impact of mirthful laughter on
neuroendocrine and immune function.

The Model

Goals:
* To enhance emotional, physical, and spiritual healing of a hospitalized person.
* To enhance emotional, physical, and spiritual support for visitors.
* To enhance emotional, physical, and spiritual support for hospital employees and providers.
* To provide a resource center for information and research on humor.

Objectives:
* To create a humor cart called "Customer Elations."
* To train volunteers to be Jocular Visitors (the JV!) by sharing the items on the cart and/or personally visiting customers.
* To provide a caring and upbeat environment for visitors as well through the use of props, puppets, stickers, and/or just a smile.
* To create bulletin boards for the units with quips, quotes, and cartoons so that the staff can laugh too.
* To collect articles from magazines and research journals on the benefits of humor and creativity.

Staffing:
* The department will be headed by the chief HA!HA!LOGIST, Jacki Kwan, LCSW-C.
* The staff will consist of trained volunteers and volunteer clowns, with total support from the entire hospital, administration, and community.
* There will be a need for a number of volunteers to organize individual humor projects (i.e. folks to organize audio and video tapes, games, humor books, cartoon albums, bulletin boards, clown attire, wigs, make-up, and maintain the inventory).

* In addition to the regular volunteer orientation, specific training will be required for the JV (jocular visitors) in using humor in a hospital setting.

Equipment:

The equipment would include a comedy cart to be called "Customer Elations," which would include funny video and audio tapes, games, cards, magic tricks, books, props, and the like. As done at Morton Plant Hospital, Plant Services would build or provide storage cabinets with locks for security.

In addition, space will be needed for an office with cabinets in which to store equipment and files and to organize the latest humor research information as well as storage of additional tapes and props that may not fit on the cart.

A separate phone extension would facilitate picking up requests specifically for a HA!HA!LOGY Maintenance Opportunity (HMO).

The Operation: (non-medically speaking)

The service provided will be free of charge and accessed by the customer, either upon admission with a form (to be developed) or by phone. The customer would either fill out the form upon admission or on the unit and give it to his or her nurse or call the HA!HA!LOGY office to request a video (or game, etc.). A volunteer would deliver the request to the room. The request would then be documented on a form (to be developed), which would have customer name, date, and item requested. The item could be borrowed for up to 24 hours.

When finished, the customer would either call the volunteer office for pick-up or return the item to the nurses' station. The unit secretary would then contact our department to notify us of the return. The customer could also request a visit from one of our volunteers (HA!HA!LOGISTS) or a clown visit, which would require 48 hours notice. Initially, the HA!HA!LOGY department hours of operation will be Monday, Wednesday, and Thursday from 12:30 p.m. to 4:30 p.m.

In addition, there would be floaters (not sinkers!) who would roam the hospital with or without the cart, making rounds – "Merry-Go-Rounds."

With the help of volunteers, we will create bulletin boards (s'moregasboards) to be posted at nurses' stations. Employees and Providers may need some levity as well! These boards will contain jokes or articles of interest, funny and/or human (humor) interest stories, and the like.

Perhaps a Humor Corner could be established in the gift shop where gag items and books on humor could be sold. Those particular items could be coded separately so that the proceeds would go to support the Division of HA!HA!LOGY.

(And now for) The Budget:

Start up costs for Morton Plant Hospital were approximately $6,000. In addition to hospital funding, specific funding requests will be submitted to local philanthropic organizations and corporations. Also, this proposal could be submitted to The HUMOR Project in Saratoga Springs, New York, which provided a start up grant to Morton Plant Hospital. At Morton Plant, the Auxiliary and the hospital, as well as donations from individuals and organizations, supports the program.

I have already received a pledge from Shayne Schneider, President of Mentor's Inc. for $500 to be earmarked for the start-up of a video library. Plus, another $1000 has been obtained from an anonymous donor. Similar individual and corporate funding will be aggressively sought upon approval of this concept.

If the Executive Committee approves this program, a detailed budget will be developed and submitted for final approval.

Getting the Word Out:
Communication is vital, not only throughout the hospital, but in the community as well. A media event could be planned for the launching of this program so that folks within and without the hospital would know that this service is available and free of charge! Kind of a Mirthday Party to celebrate the birth of the Division.

Information about the Division of HA!HA!LOGY would be distributed by flyers to all department heads in the hospital. The Chairman of HA!HA!LOGY could attend an interdepartmental meeting to describe the program and how it works.

…And Finally
"We become so overwhelmed by illness, death and grief that we forget that humor, like the moon, can bring relief to our darkest times."
Allen Klein

A lot of serious work goes on in hospitals – we know this is true. With the creation of the Division of HA!HA!LOGY, we have an opportunity to balance the gravity with levity. Hospitals can be very scary and lonely places. Positive humor and laughter may provide a respite, albeit perhaps only for a moment. Positive humor facilitates human connection.

"Laughter is the shortest distance between two people."
Victor Borge

Dr. Joel Goodman, Director of The HUMOR Project in Saratoga Springs, NY, says that humor prevents "hardening of the attitudes." What is proposed here is a harkening of the gladitudes and gratitudes for the opportunity to make a difference in the lives of every person who walks through the doors of this hospital as well as the lives of those in our community at large.

Respectfully submitted,
Jacki Kwan, LCSW-C

Start-Up Inventory and Costs for HA!HA!LOGY®

The following may help you gauge estimated costs for initiating a Humor Therapy program in a facility near you. Keep in mind that these figures are based on 2000 prices.

Description	Cost
Laughter Club Registration	$ 100
Videotapes	$ 500
Humor Library	$ 200
Stickers	$ 20
Props and Gag Items	$ 200
Miscellaneous Supplies	$ 100
Puppets	$ 200
Subscriptions for Journals	$ 250
TOTAL	$1520
Optional Items:	
TV's	$ 200 (each)
TV cart	$ 150 (each)
Humor Cart	$1000 (each)

Humor Therapy and Thearpeutic Clowning Web Sites

www.aath.org – The Association for Applied and Therapeutic Humor. The Association for Applied and Therapeutic Humor was created to educate healthcare professionals and lay audiences about the values and therapeutic uses of humor and laughter; develop, promote, conduct, and identify the need for research that further investigates the roles humor and laughter play in well-being; encourage, support, and report on innovative programs that incorporate the therapeutic use of humor; disseminate information about humor and laughter to its members through regular publications and educational opportunities; function as an interdisciplinary network for its members; and be a clearinghouse of information on humor and laughter as they relate to well-being

www.allenklein.com – the official web site for Allen Klein, the Jollytologist. Allen Klein, MA, CSP (aka "Mr. Jollytologist") is an award-winning professional speaker and best-selling author who shows audiences worldwide how to use humor to deal with not-so-funny stuff — from everyday trials and tribulations to triumphing over tragedy.

www.coai.org – Clowns of America International. An organization dedicated to the art of clowning and to bringing joy and happiness to everyone.

www.drleeberk.com – the web site of Dr. Lee Berk, a pioneer researcher studying positive emotions and their biochemical/ physiological effects in the field of Psychoneuroimmunology.

www.hospitalclown.com – go here to subscribe to the Hospital Clown Newsletter, a 16-page quarterly publication with no advertising. The Newsletter contains experiences, stories, props, routines, and articles relating to clowns in service in health care facilities and other compassionate work.

www.humorproject.com – The HUMOR Project, Inc. is the first organization in the world to focus full-time on the positive power of humor. Since 1977 their mission is to make a difference by being a unique, pioneering, and cutting-edge organization that touches the lives of individuals, organizations, and nations. They seek to help people get more smileage out of their lives and jobs by applying the practical, positive power of humor and creativity. The HUMOR Project sponsors the annual international humor conference in April and the annual international workshop in the Fall. (2002 will be the 26th annual).

The HUMOR Project also operates the Humoresources mail-order bookstore, which offers books, videos, software, and fun props to people around the world. More than two million people have attended presentations by the HUMOR Project's Speaker's Bureau in the past 25 years. For a free copy of the Humor Sourcebook, contact 518-587-8770 or write The HUMOR Project, Inc., 480 Broadway, Suite 210, Saratoga Springs, NY 12866.

www.humorx.com – the official web site for Karyn Buxman, MSN, CSP, CPAE. Karyn Buxman is one the leading national experts on therapeutic humor and puts her humor studies to work through speaking, writing, and consulting.

www.jesthealth.com – the web site for Patty Wooten and Jest for the Health of It, a company dedicated to the promotion and development of therapeutic humor skills.

www.worldlaughtertour.com – the official web site of The World Laughter Tour, founded by Steve Wilson, MA, CSP and Karyn Buxman, MSN, CSP, CPAE. This web site is the international clearinghouse for information, ideas, and news about Therapeutic Laughter and Laughter Clubs.

Other Humor Related Books
Worth Reading

The Caring Clown
by Richard Snowberg
Visual Magic
1223 S. 28th Street
La Crosse, WI 54601
$12 plus $1 s/h

***The Courage to Laugh: Humor, Hope, and Healing
in the Face of Death and Dying***
and
The Healing Power of Humor
by Allen Klein
Published by Tarcher/Putman
Available at most bookstores.

The Hospital Clown: A Closer Look
Edition 2000 by Patty Wooten and
Shobhana "Shobi" Schwebke
PO Box 8957
Emeryville, CA 94662
20 plus $4 s/h

***House Calls: How We Can All Heal the World One
Visit at a Time***
by Patch Adams, MD
Robert D. Reed Publishers
750 La Playa, Suite 647
San Francisco, CA 94121
www.rdrpublishers.com
$11.95 plus $2.50 s/h

The Joyful Journey of Hospital Clowning
by Anita Thies, Kathy Piatt, and Tammy Miller
Lighthearted Press
761 Cornwall Rd.
State College, PA 16803
lightheartedpress@email.com
$10

Almost Home
Appendix E

Other Health Related Resources and Organizations

Alliance for Aging Research
2021 K St., NW, Suite 305
Washington, DC 20006
Phone: 202-293-3856 Fax: 202-785-8574
www.agingresearch.org

Alzheimer's Association
919 N Michigan Ave., Suite 1100
Chicago, IL 60611-1676
Phone: 800-272-3900 Fax: 312-335-1100
www.alz.org

**American Association of Homes
and Services for the Aging**
2319 Connecticut Ave. NW
Washington, DC 20008-1520
Phone: 202-783-2242 Fax: 202-783-2255
www.aahsa.org

American College of Health Care Administrators
1800 Diagonal Rd., Suite 355
Alexandria, VA 22314
Phone: 888-88-ACHCA Fax: 703-739-7901
www.achca.org

American Geriatric Society
The Empire State Building
350 Fifth Ave., Suite 801
New York, NY 10118
Phone: 212-308-1414 Fax: 212-832-8646
www.americangeriatrics.org

American Health Care Association
1201 L St., NW
Washington, DC 20005
Phone: 202-842-4444 Fax: 202-842-3860
www.ahca.org

Assisted Living Federation of America
11200 Waples Mill Rd., Suite 150
Fairfax, VA 22030
Phone: 703-691-8100 Fax: 703-691-8106

National Association of Residential Care Facilities
c/o Nome Associates
55 Farmington Ave., Suite 405
Hartford, CT 06105
Phone: 860-246-8764 Fax: 860-524-8461
www.health-connect.com/narcf

National Center for Assisted Living
1201 L St. NW
Washington, DC 20005
Phone: 202-842-4444 Fax: 202-842-3860
www.ncal.org

National Citizens' Coalition for Nursing Home Reform
1424 16th St. NW, Suite 202
Washington, DC 20036
Phone: 202-332-2275 Fax: 202-332-2949
www.nccnhr.org

National Council on the Aging, Inc.
409 3rd St. SW
Washington, DC 20024
Phone: 202-479-1200 Fax: 202-479-0735
www.ncoa.org

National Hospice and Palliative Care Organization
1700 Diagonal Rd., Suite 300
Alexandria, VA 22314
Phone: 703-837-1500 Fax: 703-525-5762
www.nhpco.org

**National Investment Center for the Seniors Housing
and Care Industries**
705 Melvin Ave., Suite 201
Annapolis, MD 21401
Phone: 410-267-0504 Fax: 410-268-4620
www.nic.org

Contact Me. I'll get back to you.

Jacki Kwan, LCSW-C
PO Box 30769
Bethesda, MD 20824
email: jacki@hahalogy.com
www.hahalogy.com

Share The Journey

"Buy this book! It is written with wonder and wit from a woman whose mission is to 'change the world one HA! at a time'."
–Allen Klein, author of *The Courage to Laugh* and *The Healing Power of Humor*

Check with your leading bookstore or order here.

Almost Home   **$14.99**

Embracing The Magical Connection   x quantity   _____
Between Positive Humor & Spirituality   + shipping   _____
Maryland Residents Please Add 5% Sales Tax   + sales tax   _____

Shipping
USA: $3.95 for first book; add $2.00 for each additional book
Canada: $6.00 for first book; add $4.00 for each additional book

VISA **MasterCard**   **Order Total** (_____)

credit card # _____ expires_____
please sign _____

Paying by ___Check* ___VISA ___ MasterCard **No CODs**
* Mail to: HA!HA!Logy!®
   PO Box 30769, Bethesda, MD 20824-0769
* $30 return check fee.

For Faster Service FAX Orders To: 301-907-4610

Please Print

Name _____
Address_____
City/State/Zip_____Country_____

Phone ( )_____Email(optional)_____